Workshop on Semantic Resources and Semantic Annotation for Natural Language Processing and the Digital Humanities 2015

Held at NODALIDA 2015

NEALT Proceedings Series Volume 27

Vilnius, Lithuania
11-13 May 2015

Editors:

Bolette Sandford Pedersen
Sussi Olsen
Lars Borin

ISBN: 978-1-5108-0297-1

Printed from e-media with permission by:

Curran Associates, Inc.
57 Morehouse Lane
Red Hook, NY 12571

Some format issues inherent in the e-media version may also appear in this print version.

Printed by Curran Associates, Inc. (2015)

For permission requests, please contact the Association for Computational Linguistics at the address below.

Association for Computational Linguistics
209 N. Eighth Street
Stroudsburg, Pennsylvania 18360

Phone: 1-570-476-8006
Fax: 1-570-476-0860

acl@aclweb.org

Additional copies of this publication are available from:

Curran Associates, Inc.
57 Morehouse Lane
Red Hook, NY 12571 USA
Phone: 845-758-0400
Fax: 845-758-2634
Email: curran@proceedings.com
Web: www.proceedings.com

NEALT

Northern European Association for Language Technology

NEALT Proceedings Series Vol. 27

Proceedings of the Workshop on

Semantic Resources and Semantic Annotation for Natural Language Processing and the Digital Humanities

NODALIDA 2015

May 11-13, 2015
Institute of the Lithuanian Language

Proceedings of the workshop on

Semantic resources and semantic annotation for Natural Language Processing and the Digital Humanities

at NODALIDA 2015
Vilnius, 11th May, 2015

edited by

Bolette Sandford Pedersen, Sussi Olsen and Lars Borin

Preface

Even if language resources covering English tend to receive most attention in the LT community, recent years have shown an increased interest in developing lexical semantic resources and semantically annotated corpora of also lesser-resourced languages, including the languages in the Nordic and Baltic region. Nevertheless, high-quality semantic resources with sufficient coverage still prove to be a serious bottleneck not only in purely rule-based NLP applications but also in supervised corpus-based approaches. Also in the Digital Humanities there is an increased interest in and need for semantic annotation which would enable more refined search in, and better visualization and analyses of large-scale corpus data.

This workshop focuses in particular on the interplay between lexical-semantic resources as resembled by wordnets, framenets, propbanks, and others and their relation to practical corpus annotation. The workshop – a follow-up on the successful Nodalida 2009 and 2013 workshops on semantic resources – intends to bring together researchers involved in building and integrating semantic resources (lexicons and corpora) as well as researchers who apply these resources for semantic processing. Also researchers who are more theoretically interested in investigating the interplay between lexical semantics, lexicography, corpus linguistics and Digital Humanities are welcome.

For the workshop we invited papers presenting original research relating to semantic resources for NLP and DH on topics such as:

- representation of lexical-semantic knowledge for computational use
- the interplay between lexical-semantic resources and semantically annotated corpora
- corpus-based approaches to lexical-semantic resources
- tools for semantic annotation
- terminology and lexical semantics: concept-based vs lexical semantic approaches
- monolingual vs. multilingual approaches to semantic lexicons and corpora
- quality assessment of lexical-semantic resources: criteria, methods
- applications using lexical-semantic resources (information retrieval, semantic tagging of corpora, MT, Digital Humanities etc.)
- machine-learning techniques to discover semantic structures such as unsupervised learning, distance supervision, or cross-language learning.
- traditional lexicography and NLP lexicons: re-use and differences
- applying semantic resources (lexica, corpora) for semantic processing
- word sense disambiguation based on lexically informed techniques

We received a total of 7 submissions, each of which was reviewed by at least two (anonymous) members of the program committee (see below). On the basis of the reviews, 5 submissions were accepted for presentation at the workshop and inclusion in the workshop proceedings (subject to revisions required by the reviewers).

The workshop was designed to be a highly interactive event. After an invited oral presentation by Johan Bos (University of Groningen): – *Issues in parallel meaning banking* – the other contributions to the workshop were presented during two oral sessions. A general discussion concluded the workshop.

Bolette Sandford Pedersen, Sussi Olsen and Lars Borin 2015. Preface. *Proceedings of the workshop on Semantic resources and semantic annotation for Natural Language Processing and the Digital Humanities at NODALIDA 2015*. NEALT Proceedings Series 27 / Linköping Electronic Conference Proceedings 112: i–ii.

Workshop organizers

- Bolette Sandford Pedersen (University of Copenhagen, Organizing Chair)
- Lars Borin (University of Gothenburg)
- Markus Forsberg (University of Gothenburg)
- Sanni Nimb (Association for Danish Language and Literature)
- Anders Søgaard (University of Copenhagen)
- Pierre Nugues (Lund University)
- Hector Martinez Alonso (University of Copenhagen)
- Anders Johannsen (University of Copenhagen)
- Sussi Olsen (University of Copenhagen)

Program committee

- Lars Borin (University of Gothenburg)
- Normunds Grūzītis (University of Gothenburg)
- Eiríkur Rögnvaldsson (Iceland University)
- Ruth Vatvedt Fjeld (University of Oslo)
- Markus Forsberg (University of Gothenburg)
- Karin Friberg Heppin (University of Gothenburg)
- Richard Johansson (University of Gothenburg)
- Rune Lain Knudsen (University of Oslo)
- Dimitrios Kokkinakis (University of Gothenburg)
- André Lynum (University of Oslo)
- Sanni Nimb (Association for Danish Language and Literature)
- Pierre Nugues (Lund University)
- Krister Lindén (University of Helsinki)
- Jussi Piitulainen (University of Helsinki)
- Bolette Sandford Pedersen (University of Copenhagen)
- Anders Søgaard (University of Copenhagen)
- Joel Priestley (University of Oslo)
- Heili Orav (University of Tartu)
- Esben Alfort (Ankiro, Denmark)
- Jørg Asmussen, (Association for Danish Language and Literature)
- Hector Martinez Alonso, (University of Copenhagen)
- Anders Johannsen, (University of Copenhagen)

Contents

Here be dragons?
The perils and promises of inter-resource lexical-semantic mapping

Lars Borin **Luis Nieto Piña** **Richard Johansson**

Språkbanken, Department of Swedish, University of Gothenburg, Sweden
{lars.borin, luis.nieto.pina, richard.johansson}@svenska.gu.se

Abstract

Lexical-semantic knowledges sources are a stock item in the language technologist's toolbox, having proved their practical worth in many and diverse natural language processing (NLP) applications.

In linguistics, lexical semantics comes in many flavors, but in the NLP world, wordnets reign more or less supreme. There has been some promising work utilizing Roget-style thesauruses instead, but wider experimentation is hampered by the limited availability of such resources.

The work presented here is a first step in the direction of creating a freely available Roget-style lexical resource for modern Swedish. Here, we explore methods for automatic disambiguation of inter-resource mappings with the longer-term goal of utilizing similar techniques for automatic enrichment of lexical-semantic resources.

1 Introduction

1.1 The uniformity of lexical semantic resources for NLP

Lexical-semantic knowledges sources are a stock item in the language technologist's toolbox, having proved their practical worth in many and diverse natural language processing (NLP) applications.

Although lexical semantics and the closely related field of lexical typology have long been large and well-researched branches of linguistics (see, e.g., Cruse 1986; Goddard 2001; Murphy 2003; Vanhove 2008), the lexical-semantic knowledge source of choice for NLP applications is WordNet (Fellbaum, 1998b), a resource which arguably has been built largely in isolation from the linguistic mainstream and which thus is somewhat disconnected from it.

However, the English-language Princeton WordNet (PWN) and most wordnets for other languages are freely available, often broad-coverage lexical resources, which goes a long way toward explaining their popularity and wide usage in NLP as due at least in part to a kind of streetlight effect.

For this reason, we should certainly endeavor to explore other kinds of lexical-semantic resources as components in NLP applications. This is easier said than done, however. The PWN is a manually built resource, and efforts aiming at automatic creation of similar resources for other languages on the basis of PWN, such as Universal WordNet (de Melo and Weikum, 2009) or BabelNet (Navigli and Ponzetto, 2012), although certainly useful and laudable, by their very nature will simply reproduce the WordNet structure, although for a different language or languages. Of course, the same goes for the respectable number of manually constructed wordnets for other languages.[1]

Manually built alternatives to wordnets are afflicted by being for some other language than English (e.g., SALDO: Borin et al. 2013) or by not being freely available – see the next section – or possibly both.

1.2 Roget's *Thesaurus* and NLP

While wordnets completely dominate the NLP field, outside it the most well-known lexical-semantic resource for English is without doubt Roget's *Thesaurus* (also alternately referred to as "Roget" below; Roget 1852; Hüllen 2004), which appeared in its first edition in 1852 and has since been published in a large number of editions all over the English-speaking world. Although – perhaps unjustifiedly – not as well-known in NLP

[1] See the *Global WordNet Association* website: <http://globalwordnet.org>.

Lars Borin, Richard Johansson and Luis Nieto Piña 2015. Here be dragons? The perils and promises of inter-resource lexical-semantic mapping. *Proceedings of the workshop on Semantic resources and semantic annotation for Natural Language Processing and the Digital Humanities at NODALIDA 2015*. NEALT Proceedings Series 27 / Linköping Electronic Conference Proceedings 112: 1–11.

as the PWN, the digital version of Roget offers a valuable complement to PWN (Jarmasz and Szpakowicz, 2004), which has seen a fair amount of use in NLP (e.g., Morris and Hirst 1991; Jobbins and Evett 1995; Jobbins and Evett 1998; Wilks 1998; Kennedy and Szpakowicz 2008).

It has been proposed in the literature that Roget-style thesauruses could provide an alternative source of lexical-semantic information, which can be used both to attack other kinds of NLP tasks than a wordnet, and even work better for some of the same tasks, e.g., *lexical cohesion*, *synonym identification*, *pseudo-word-sense disambiguation*, and *analogy problems* (Morris and Hirst, 1991; Jarmasz and Szpakowicz, 2004; Kennedy and Szpakowicz, 2008; Kennedy and Szpakowicz, 2014).

An obstacle to the wider use of Roget in NLP applications is its limited availability. The only free digital version is the 1911 American edition available through Project Gutenberg.[2] This version is obviously not well suited for processing modern texts. Szpakowicz and his colleagues at the University of Ottawa have conducted a number of experiments with a modern (from 1987) edition of Roget (e.g., Jarmasz and Szpakowicz 2004; Kennedy and Szpakowicz 2008, but as far as we can tell, this dataset is not generally available, due to copyright restrictions. The work reported by Kennedy and Szpakowicz (2014) represents an effort to remedy this situation, utilizing corpus-based measures of semantic relatedness for adding new entries to both the 1911 and 1987 editions of Roget.

In order to investigate systematically the strengths and weaknesses of diverse lexical-semantic resources when applied to different classes of NLP tasks, we would need access to resources that are otherwise comparable, e.g., with respect to language, vocabulary and domain coverage. The resources should also ideally be freely available, in order to ensure reproducibility as well as to stimulate their widest possible application to a broad range of NLP problems. Unfortunately, this situation is rarely encountered in practice; for English, the experiments contrasting WordNet and Roget have indicated that these resources are indeed complementary. It would be desirable to replicate these findings, e.g., for other languages and also using lexical-semantic resources with different structures (WordNet and Roget being two out of a large number of possibilities).

This is certainly a central motivation for the work presented here, the ultimate goal of which is to develop automatic methods for producing or considerably facilitating the production of a Swedish counterpart of Roget with a large and up-to-date vocabulary coverage. This is not to be done by translation, as in previous work by de Melo and Weikum (2008) and Borin et al. (2014). Instead, an existing but largely outdated Roget-style thesaurus will provide the scaffolding, where new word senses can be inserted with the help of two different kinds of semantic relatedness measures:

1. One such measure is corpus-based, similar to the experiments conducted by Kennedy and Szpakowicz (2014), described above.
2. The other measure utilizes an existing lexical-semantic resource (SALDO: Borin et al. 2013).

In the latter case, we also have a more theoretical aim with our work. SALDO was originally conceived as an "associative thesaurus" (Lönngren, 1998), and even though its organization in many respects differs significantly from that of Roget, there are also some commonalities. Hence, our hypothesis is that the structure of SALDO will yield a good semantic relatedness measure for the task at hand. SALDO is described in Section 2.2 below.

2 The datasets

2.1 Bring's Swedish thesaurus

Sven Casper Bring (1842–1931) was the originator of the first and so far only adaptation of Roget's *Thesaurus* to Swedish, which appeared in 1930 under the title *Svenskt Ordförråd ordnat i begreppsklasser* 'Swedish vocabulary arranged in conceptual classes' (referred to as "Bring" or "Bring's thesaurus" below). The work itself consists of two parts: (1) a conceptually organized list of Roget categories; and (2) an alphabetically ordered lemma index.

In addition, there is a brief preface by S. C. Bring, which we reproduce here in its entirety:[3]

[2]See <http://www.gutenberg.org/ebooks/22> and Cassidy (2000).

[3]This English translation comes from the Bring resource page at Språkbanken: <http://spraakbanken.gu.se/eng/resource/bring>.

> This wordlist has been modelled on P. M. Roget's "Thesaurus of English Words and Phrases". This kind of wordlist can be seen as a synonym dictionary of sorts. But each conceptual class comprises not only synonyms, but words of all kinds which are habitually used in discoursing on the kind of topics which could be subsumed under the class label concept, understood in a wide sense.
>
> Regarding Roget's classification system, there are arguably a number of classes which ought to be merged or split. But this classification seems to have established itself solidly through many editions of Roget's work as well as German copies of it. It should also be considered an advantage that the same classification is used in such dictionaries for different languages.
>
> Uppsala in September 1930.
>
> *S. C. Bring*

Like in Roget, the vocabulary included in Bring is divided into slightly over 1,000 "conceptual classes". A "conceptual class" corresponds to what is usually referred to as a "head" in the literature on Roget. Each conceptual class consists of a list of words (lemmas), subdivided first into nouns, verbs and others (mainly adjectives, adverbs and phrases), and finally into paragraphs. In the paragraphs, the distance – expressed as difference in list position – between words provides a rough measure of their semantic distance.

Bring thus forms a hierarchical structure with four levels:

(1) conceptual class (Roget "head")
(2) part of speech
(3) paragraph
(4) lemma (word sense)

This stands in contrast to Roget, where the formal structure defines a nine-level hierarchy (Jarmasz and Szpakowicz, 2001; Jarmasz and Szpakowicz, 2004):

(1) class
(2) section
(3) subsection
(4) category, or head group
(5) head (Bring "conceptual class")
(6) part of speech
(7) paragraph
(8) semicolon group
(9) lemma (word sense)

Since most of the Bring classes have corresponding heads in Roget, it should be straightforward to add the levels above Roget heads/Bring classes to Bring if needed. There are some indications in the literature that this additional structure can in fact be useful for calculating semantic similarity (Jarmasz and Szpakowicz, 2004).

Bring's thesaurus has recently been made available in two digital versions by Språkbanken (the Swedish Language Bank) at the University of Gothenburg, both versions under a Creative Commons Attribution License:

Bring (v. 1): A digital version of the full contents of the original 1930 book version (148,846 entries).[4]

Blingbring (v. 0.1), a version of Bring where obsolete items have been removed and the remaining entries have been provided with word sense identifiers from SALDO (see section 2.2), providing links to most of Språkbanken's other lexical resources. This version contains 126,911 entries.[5]

The linking to SALDO senses in the current Blingbring version (v 0.1) has not involved a disambiguation step. Rather, it has been made by matching lemma-POS combinations from the two resources. For this reason, Blingbring includes slightly over 21,000 ambiguous entries (out of approximately 127,000 in total), or about 4,800 ambiguous word sense assignments (out of about 43,000 unique lemma-POS combinations).

The aim of the experiments described below has been to assess the feasibility of disambiguating these ambiguous linkages automatically, and specifically also to evaluate SALDO as a possible knowledge source for accomplishing this disambiguation. The longer-term goal of this work is to develop good methods for adding modern vocabulary automatically to Bring from, e.g., SALDO, thereby hopefully producing a modern Swedish Roget-style resource for the NLP community.

2.2 SALDO

SALDO (Borin et al., 2013) is a large (137K entries and 2M wordforms) morphological and lexical-semantic lexicon for modern Swedish, freely available (under a Creative Commons Attribution license).[6]

As a lexical-semantic resource, SALDO is organized very differently from a wordnet (Borin and Forsberg, 2009). As mentioned above, it was initially conceived as an "associative thesaurus".

[4] <http://spraakbanken.gu.se/eng/resource/bring>

[5] <http://spraakbanken.gu.se/eng/resource/blingbring>

[6] <http://spraakbanken.gu.se/eng/resource/saldo>

Since it has been extended following the principles laid down initially by Lönngren (1998), this characterization should still be valid, even though it has grown tremendously over the last decade.

If the fundamental organizing principle of PWN is the idea of full synonyms in a taxonomic concept hierarchy, the basic linguistic idea underlying SALDO is instead that, semantically speaking, the whole vocabulary of a language can be described as having a center – or core – and (consequently) a periphery. The notion of *core vocabulary* is familiar from several linguistic subdisciplines (Borin, 2012). In SALDO this idea is consistently applied down to the level of individual word senses, as we will now describe.

The basic lexical-semantic organizational principle of SALDO is hierarchical. Every entry in SALDO – representing a word sense – is supplied with one or more semantic descriptors, which are themselves also entries in the dictionary. All entries in SALDO are actually occurring words or conventionalized or lexicalized multi-word units of the language. No attempt is made to fill perceived gaps in the lexical network using definition-like paraphrases, as is sometimes done in PWN (Fellbaum, 1998a, 5f). A further difference as compared to PWN (and Roget-style thesuruses) is that SALDO aims to provide a lexical-semantic description of *all* the words of the language, including the closed-class items (prepositions, subjunctions, interjections, etc.), and also including many proper nouns.

One of the semantic descriptors in SALDO, called *primary*, is obligatory. The primary descriptor is the entry which better than any other entry fulfills two requirements: (1) it is a semantic neighbor of the entry to be desribed and (2) it is more central than it. However, there is no requirement that the primary descriptor is of the same part of speech as the entry itself. Thus, the primary descriptor of *kniv* 'knife (n)' is *skära* 'cut (v)', and that of *lager* 'layer (n)' is *på* 'on (p)'.

Through the primary descriptors SALDO is a single tree, rooted by assigning an artifical top sense (called PRIM) as primary descriptor to the 41 topmost word senses.

That two words are semantic neighbors means that there is a direct semantic relationship between them (such as synonymy, hyponymy, meronymy, argument-predicate relationship, etc.). As could be seen from the examples given above, SALDO includes not only open-class words, but also pronouns, prepositions, conjunctions etc. In such cases closeness must sometimes be determined with respect to function or syntagmatic connections, rather than ("word-semantic") content.

Centrality is determined by means of several criteria: frequency, stylistic value, word formation, and traditional lexical-semantic relations all combine to determine which of two semantically neighboring words is to be considered more central.

For more details of the organization of SALDO and the linguistic motivation underlying it, see Borin et al. (2013).

Like Roget, SALDO has a kind of topical structure, which – again like Roget, but different from a wordnet – includes and connects lexical items of different parts of speech, but its topology is characterized by a much deeper hierarchy than that found in Roget. There are no direct correspondences in SALDO to the lexical-semantic relations making up a wordnet (minimally synonymy and – part-of-speech internal – hyponymy).

Given the (claimed) thesaural character of SALDO, we would expect a SALDO-based semantic similarity measure to work well for disambiguating the ambiguous Blingbring entries, and not be inferior to a corpus-based or wordnet-based measure. There is no sufficiently large Swedish wordnet at present, so for now we must restrict ourselves to a comparison of a corpus-based and a SALDO-based method.

The experiments described below were conducted using SALDO v. 2.3 as available for downloading on Språkbanken's website.

3 Automatic disambiguation of ambiguous Bring entries

We now turn to the question of automatically linking the Bring and SALDO lexicons: many entries in Bring have more than one sense in SALDO, and we present a number of methods to automatically rank SALDO senses by how well they fit into a particular Bring class. Specifically, since entries in Bring are not specified in terms of a sense, this allows us to predict the SALDO sense that is most appropriate for a given Bring entry. For instance, the lexicon lists the noun *broms* as belonging to Bring class 366, which contains a large number of terms related to animals. SALDO defines two senses for this word: *broms-1* 'brake' and *broms-2* 'horsefly', but it is only the second sense that should be listed in this Bring class.

In this work we consider the task of selecting a SALDO sense for a Bring entry, but we imagine that the methods proposed here can be applied in other scenarios as well. For instance, it is possible that they could allow us to predict the Bring class for a word that is *not* listed in Bring, but we leave this task for future investigation. The methods are related to those presented by Johansson (2014) for automatically suggesting FrameNet frames for SALDO entries.

We first describe how we use the SALDO network and cooccurrence statistics from corpora to represent the meaning of SALDO entries. These meaning representations are then used to carry out the disambiguation. We investigate two distinct ways to use the representations for disambiguating: (1) by selecting a *prototype* (centroid) for each class, and then selecting the SALDO sense that is most similar to the prototype; (2) by using the existing Bring entries as training instances for a *classifier* that assigns a Bring class to a SALDO entry, and then ranking the SALDO senses by the probability output by the classifier when considering each sense for a Bring class.

3.1 Representing the meaning of a SALDO entry

To be able to connect a SALDO entry to a Bring class, we must represent its *meaning* in some structured way, in order to relate it to other entries with a similar meaning. There are two broad approaches to representing word meaning in NLP work: representations based on the structure of a formal knowledge representation (in our case the SALDO network), and those derived from cooccurrence statistics in corpora (*distributional* representations). In this work, we explore both options.

3.1.1 Word senses in Bring and in SALDO

But even if we restrict ourselves to how they are conceived in the linguistic literature, word senses are finicky creatures. They are obviously language-dependent, strongly so if we are to believe, e.g., Goddard (2001). Furthermore, there seems to be a strong element of tradition – or ideology – informing assumptions about how word senses contribute to the interpretation of complex linguistic items, such as productive derivations, compounds and incorporating constructions, as well as phrases and clauses. This in turn determines the granularity – the degree of polysemy – posited for lexical entries.

One thing that seems to be assumed about Roget – and which if true consequently ought to hold for Bring as well – is that multiple occurrences of the same lemma (with the same part of speech) represent different word senses (e.g., Kwong 1998; Nastase and Szpakowicz 2001). This is consistent with a "splitting" approach to polysemy, similar to that exhibited by PWN and more generally by an Anglo-Saxon lexicographical tradition.

However, this is not borne out by the Bring–SALDO linking. First, there are many unambiguous – in the sense of having been assigned only one SALDO word sense – Bring lemma-POS combinations that appear in multiple Bring classes. Second, during the practical disambiguation work conducted in order to prepare the evaluation dataset for the experiments described below, the typical case was not – as would have been expected if the above assumption were correct – that ambiguous items occurring in several Bring classes would receive different word sense assignments. On the contrary, this turned out to be very much a minor phenomenon.

A "word sense" is not a well-defined notion (Kilgarriff, 1997; Hanks, 2000; Erk, 2010; Hanks, 2013), and it may well be simply that this is what we are seeing here. Specifically, the Swedish lexicographical tradition to which SALDO belongs reflects a "lumping" view on word sense discrimination. If we aspire to link resources such as Roget, Bring, SALDO, etc. between languages, issues such as this need to be resolved one way or another, so there is clearly need for more research here.

3.1.2 Lexicon-based representation

In a structure-based meaning representation, the meaning of a concept is defined by its relative position in the SALDO network. How do we operationalize this position as a practical meaning representation that can be used to compute similarity of meaning or exemplify meaning for a machine learning algorithm? It seems clear that the way this operationalization is carried out has implications for the ability of automatic systems to generalize from the set of SALDO entries associated with a Bring class, in order to reason about new entries.

When using a semantic network, the meaning of a word sense s is defined by how it is related to other word senses; in SALDO, the immediate neighborhood of s consists of a primary descriptor and possibly a set of secondary descriptors, and the meaning of s can be further analyzed by following primary and secondary edges in the SALDO graph. In this work, we follow the approach by Johansson (2014) and let the lexicon-based meaning representation $\phi(s)$ of a SALDO entry s be defined in terms of the transitive closure of the primary descriptor relation. That is, it consists of all SALDO entries observed when traversing the SALDO graph by following primary descriptor edges from s to the SALDO root entry (excluding the root itself). For instance, the meaning of the fourth sense of *fil* 'file (n)' would be represented as the set

ϕ(*fil-4*) = { *fil-4* '(computer) file (n)', *datorminne-1* 'computer memory (n)', *datalagring-1* 'data storage (n)', *lagring-1* 'storage (n)', *lagra-1* 'store (v)', *lager-2* 'stock/store (n)', *förråd-1* 'store (n)', *förvara-1* 'store/keep (v)', *ha-1* 'have (v)' }.

Computationally, these sets are implemented as high-dimensional sparse vectors, which we normalize to unit length. Although in this work we do not explicitly use the notion of similarity functions, we note that the cosine similarity applied to this representation gives rise to a network-based measure similar in spirit to that proposed by Wu and Palmer (1994):

$$\text{sim}(s_1, s_2) = \frac{|\phi(s_1) \cap \phi(s_2)|}{\sqrt{|\phi(s_1)|} \cdot \sqrt{|\phi(s_2)|}}$$

3.1.3 Corpus-based representation

Corpus-based meaning representations rely on the distributional hypothesis, which assumes that words occurring in a similar set of contexts are also similar in meaning (Harris, 1954). This intuition has been realized in a very large number of algorithms and implementations (Turney and Pantel, 2010), and the result of applying such a model is typically that word meaning is modeled *geometrically* by representing co-occurrence statistics in a vector space: this makes it straightforward to define similarity and distance measures using standard vector-space metrics, e.g. the Euclidean distance or the cosine similarity. In this work, we applied the skip-gram model by Mikolov et al. (2013), which considers co-occurrences of each word in the corpus with other words in a small window; this model has proven competitive in many evaluations, including the frame prediction task described by Johansson (2014).

Since our goal is to select a word sense defined by SALDO, but corpus-based meaning representation methods typically do not distinguish between senses, we applied the postprocessing algorithm developed by Johansson and Nieto Piña (2015) to convert vectors produced by the skip-gram model into new vectors representing SALDO senses. For instance, this allows us to say that for the Swedish noun *fil*, the third sense defined in SALDO ('sour milk') is geometrically close to *milk* and *yoghurt* while the fourth sense ('computer file') is close to *program* and *memory*. This algorithm decomposes vector-based word meaning representations into a convex combination of several components, each representing a sense defined by a semantic network such as SALDO. The vector representations of senses are selected so that they minimize the geometric distances to their neighbors in the SALDO graph. The authors showed that the decomposed representations can be used for predicting FrameNet frames for a SALDO sense.

3.2 Disambiguating by comparing to a prototype

The fact that corpus-based representations for SALDO senses are located in a real-valued vector space allows us to generate a prototype for a certain Bring conceptual class by means of averaging the sense vectors belonging to a that class in Bring. This prototype is in the same vector space that the sense representations, so we are able to measure distances between sense vectors and prototypes and determine which sense is closer to the concept embodied in the class prototype.

Thus, our first method for disambiguating links between Bring items and SALDO senses works as follows. For each class j, a prototype c_j is calculated by averaging those sense vectors v_i that are unambiguously linked to a Bring item b_i from class j:

$$c_j = \frac{1}{n} \sum_{b_i \in j} v_i$$

where n is the number of unambiguous links in class j.

Then, for an ambiguous link between a Bring item b_k in class j and its set of possible vectors $\{v_{kl}\}$, the distance from each vector to the class centroid c_j is measured, and the closest one is selected as the representation of the SALDO sense linked to b_k:

$$\arg\min_{l} \mathrm{d}(c_j, v_{kl})$$

where d is a distance function. In our case we have chosen to use *cosine distance*, which is commonly applied on the kind of representations obtained from the skip-gram model (Mikolov et al., 2013) to compute similarity between representations.

3.3 Disambiguating with classifiers

Statistical classifiers offer a wide range of options to learn the distribution of labeled data, which afterwards can be used to label unseen data instances. They are not constrained to work with data in a geometric space, as opposed to the method explained in the previous section. Thus, we can apply classifiers on lexicon-based representations as well.

In our case, we are not interested so much in classifying new instances as in assessing the confidence of such classifications. Consequently, in our ambiguous data we have a set of instances that can possibly be linked to a Bring entry whose class is known to us. Therefore, we would like to ascertain how confident a classifier is when assigning these instances to their corresponding class, and base our decision to disambiguate the link on this information.

For this task we use the Python library Scikit-learn (Pedregosa et al., 2011), a general machine learning package which offers a variety of statistical classifiers. Specifically, we work with a logistic regression method (instantiated with the library's default values, except the inverse regularization strength, set to 100), which classifies instances based on the probability that they belong to each possible class.

The classifier is trained on the set of SALDO sense vectors unambiguously linked to Bring items and their conceptual class information. Once trained, it can be given a set of SALDO sense representations $\{v_{kl}\}$ ambiguously assigned to one Bring entry b_k in class j and, instead of simply classifying them, output their probabilities $\{p_{jl}\}$ of belonging to class j. We then only have to select the sense with the highest probability to disambiguate the link:

$$\arg\max_{l} p_{jl}$$

4 Experiments

4.1 Evaluation data preparation

The Blingbring data was downloaded from Språkbanken's website and a sample of ambiguous Bring–SALDO linkages was selected for manual disambiguation.

An initial sample was drawn from this data set according to the following principles:[7]

- The sampling unit was the class+part of speech-combination, i.e., *nouns in class 12*, *verbs in class 784*, etc.
- This unit had to contain at least 100 lemmas (actual range: 100–569 lemmas),
- out of which at least 1 must be unambiguous (actual range: 56–478 unambiguous lemmas),
- and at least 4 had to be ambiguous.
- From the ambiguous lemmas, 4 were randomly selected (using the Python function `random-sample`).

The goal was to produce an evaluation set of approximately 1,000 items, and this procedure yielded 1,008 entries to be disambiguated. The disambiguation was carried out by the first author. In practice, it deviated from the initial procedure and proceeded more opportunistically, since reference often had to be made to the main dataset in order to determine the correct SALDO word sense. On these occasions, it was often convenient to (a) either disambiguate additional items in the same Bring class; and/or (b) disambiguate the same items throughout the entire dataset.

In the end, 1,368 entries were disambiguated for the experiments, out of which about 500 came out of the original sample. The degree of ambiguity in this gold standard data is shown in the second column of Table 1, while the third column shows the degree of ambiguity in the full Blingbring dataset containing 44,615 unique lemma-POS combinations.

On the other hand, unambiguous entries in Blingbring linking one Bring item to one SALDO sense are isolated to serve as training data. As mentioned above in Section 3.1.1, the structure of Bring's thesaurus makes it possible for a word to appear in more than one conceptual class; if the

[7] These should be seen as first-approximation heuristic principles, and not based on any more detailed analysis of the data. We expect that further experiments will provide better data on which to base such decisions.

# senses/ entry	GS data: # entries	Blingbring: # entries
1	–	39,275
2	888	4,006
3	266	873
4	122	286
5	56	102
6	18	31
7	10	18
8	7	10
9	1	3
10	–	6
11	–	5

Table 1: Word-sense ambiguity in the gold standard data and in Blingbring

Method	Accuracy
Random baseline	0.4238
Corpus-based, incl. overlap	0.5731
Corpus-based, no overlap	0.5651

Table 2: Disambiguation accuracy using a similarity measure.

PoS	Proportion	Accuracy
Noun	54.8%	0.5819
Verb	21.3%	0.5538
Others	23.2%	0.5485

Table 3: Disambiguation accuracy by Part-of-Speech using a similarity measure. Overlapping instances included in the training set.

SALDO sense related to those two or more instances is the same, we may have a training instance that spans more than just one class. Initially, it may seem reasonable to exclude such instances from the training data, as their presence may be problematic for the definition of a class. But this phenomenon is quite ubiquitous: 72.6% of the senses unambiguously associated with a Bring entry in Blingbring appear in more than one class. For this reason, we define two different training sets, one that includes *overlap* among the classes and one that does not, and conduct conduct experiments separately on each of them.

4.2 Prototype-based disambiguation

In this section we give the results obtained with the method described in Section 3.2. This experiment is performed using corpus-based representations only, as lexicon-based ones lack a geometrical interpretation, on which the cosine similarity measure used is based.

Table 2 lists the accuracy of the method on our evaluation set. Two results are given corresponding to the training set containing or not instances that span several classes. The accuracy of a random baseline is also given as a reference. Both of the approaches have an accuracy well above the random baseline with an improvement of over 0.14 points, and we observe that there is practically no difference between them, although the approach in which instances overlapping classes are included in the training data performs slightly better.

In Table 3 we present for this last case a breakdown of the accuracy into the parts of speech that Bring classes list: *nouns*, *verbs* and *others*.[8] The table also lists the proportions of these classes in the data. No significant difference can be appreciated between the diverse types of words, although nouns fare slightly better than the other two cases.

4.3 Classification-based disambiguation

The results of applying the method introduced in Section 3.3 are given here. In this experiment we also consider lexicon-based data besides the corpus-based representations.

Table 4 lists the accuracies obtained in each instance: corpus-based or lexicon-based data, using either overlapping instances or not. The random baseline accuracy is also shown for reference.

In this case, we observe a greater improvement over the baseline than in the previous experiment with an increase in accuracy of 0.23 between the best cases in each experiment. There is also a considerable difference between the two types of data: the best case using lexicon-based representations provides an accuracy improvement of 0.12 over the best result obtained with corpus-based data. Contrary to the experience of the previous experiment, there is a substantial difference between the presence or absence of overlapping instances in the training data: the accuracy increases by 0.03 in the case of corpus-based data when overlapping instances are used, and by 0.13 in the case of lexicon-based data. This behaviour may seem

[8] As explained in Section 2.1, the tag *others* encompasses mainly adjectives, adverbs and phrases, and unfortunately there is not enough information in Bring to separate these classes and give a more fine-grained analysis.

Method	Accuracy
Random baseline	0.4238
Corpus-based, incl. overlap	0.6879
Corpus-based, no overlap	0.6572
Lexicon-based, incl. overlap	0.7836
Lexicon-based, no overlap	0.6499

Table 4: Disambiguation accuracy using a classifier.

PoS	Accuracy
Corpus-based representations	
Noun	0.7372
Verb	0.6308
Others	0.5825
Lexicon-based representations	
Noun	0.7885
Verb	0.8154
Others	0.7282

Table 5: Disambiguation accuracy by Part-of-Speech using a classifier. Overlapping instances included in the training data.

counter-intuitive, since using training instances that belong to more than one class should dilute the boundaries between those classes. It should be noted here, however, that, given a new instance, the main task assigned in our problem to the classifier is not to decide to which class the instance belongs (as this information is already known), but to output the membership probability for a certain class, so that we are able to compare with those of other instances. Thus, the boundaries between classes matter less to us than the amount of training data that allows the classifier to learn the definition of each class separately.

Table 5 presents an accuracy breakdown for the highest scoring approach in the previous results (i.e., including overlap) using each type of data. These results also differ from the ones in the previous experiments, as we observe a marked difference between parts of speech: using corpus-based representations, nouns obtain the highest accuracy with 0.10 points over the other two classes, while using lexicon based data favours verbs, although closely followed by nouns.

5 Conclusions and future work

Summing up the main results, (1) both the corpus-based and the lexicon-based methods resulted in a significantly higher disambiguation accuracy compared to the random baseline; (2) contrary to intuition, using overlapping instances yielded better accuracy than using only non-overlapping items, which we attribute to the increased amount of training data in the former case; and (3) the hypothesis that the SALDO-based method would yield a better result was supported by the experiments.

The results of the lexicon-based method are already good enough overall that it will be possible to use it as a preprocessing step in order to speed up the disambiguation of the remaining ambiguous entries considerably. The results could also be analyzed in more detail in order to find out whether there are special cases that could be automatically identified where the accuracy may be even higher.

For instance, it would be useful to see whether the structure of the thesaurus can be used in a more sophisticated way. In this work we have only considered the top-level Bring class when selecting among the alternative SALDO senses for an ambiguous Bring entry, but as described in Section 2.1, the thesaurus is organized hierarchically, and closely related terms are placed near each other on the page.

In future work, we would like to investigate to what extent the methods that we have proposed here can be generalized to other Bring-related tasks. In particular, it would be useful to propose a Bring class for words in SALDO that are not listed in Bring, for instance because the word did not exist when the Bring lexicon was compiled. This would make a new and very useful lexical-semantic resource available for use in sophisticated Swedish NLP applications.

Acknowledgements

This research was funded by the Swedish Research Council under the grants *Towards a knowledge-based culturomics* (dnr 2012-5738), *Distributional methods to represent the meaning of frames and constructions* (dnr 2013-4944), and *Swedish FrameNet++* (dnr 2010-6013). We also acknowledge the University of Gothenburg for its support of the Centre for Language Technology and Språkbanken.

References

Lars Borin and Markus Forsberg. 2009. All in the family: A comparison of SALDO and WordNet. In *Proceedings of the Nodalida 2009 Workshop on WordNets and other Lexical Semantic Resources*, Odense.

Lars Borin, Markus Forsberg, and Lennart Lönngren. 2013. SALDO: a touch of yin to WordNet's yang. *Language Resources and Evaluation*, 47(4):1191–1211.

Lars Borin, Jens Allwood, and Gerard de Melo. 2014. Bring vs. MTRoget: Evaluating automatic thesaurus translation. In *Proceedings of LREC 2014*, pages 2115–2121, Reykjavík. ELRA.

Lars Borin. 2012. Core vocabulary: A useful but mystical concept in some kinds of linguistics. In Diana Santos, Krister Lindén, and Wanjiku Ng'ang'a, editors, *Shall we play the Festschrift game? Essays on the occasion of Lauri Carlson's 60th birthday*, pages 53–65. Springer, Berlin.

Patrick Cassidy. 2000. An investigation of the semantic relations in the Roget's Thesaurus: Preliminary results. In *Proceedings of CICLing 2000*, pages 181–204.

D. Alan Cruse. 1986. *Lexical semantics*. Cambridge University Press, Cambridge.

Gerard de Melo and Gerhard Weikum. 2008. Mapping Roget's Thesaurus and WordNet to French. In *Proceedings of LREC 2008*, Marrakech. ELRA.

Gerard de Melo and Gerhard Weikum. 2009. Towards a universal wordnet by learning from combined evidence. In *Proceedings of the 18th ACM Conference on Information and Knowledge Management (CIKM 2009)*, pages 513–522, New York. ACM.

Katrin Erk. 2010. What is word meaning, really? (And how can distributional models help us describe it?). In *Proceedings of the 2010 Workshop on GEometrical Models of Natural Language Semantics*, pages 17–26, Uppsala. ACL.

Christiane Fellbaum. 1998a. Introduction. In Christiane Fellbaum, editor, *WordNet: An electronic lexical database*, pages 1–19. MIT Press, Cambridge, Mass.

Christiane Fellbaum, editor. 1998b. *WordNet: An electronic lexical database*. MIT Press, Cambridge, Mass.

Cliff Goddard. 2001. Lexico-semantic universals: A critical overview. *Linguistic Typology*, 5:1–65.

Patrick Hanks. 2000. Do word meanings exist? *Computers and the Humanities*, 34(1–2):205–215.

Patrick Hanks. 2013. *Lexical analysis. Norms and exploitations*. MIT Press, Cambridge, Massachusetts.

Zellig Harris. 1954. Distributional structure. *Word*, 10(23).

Werner Hüllen. 2004. *A history of Roget's Thesaurus: Origins, development, and design*. Oxford University Press, Oxford.

Mario Jarmasz and Stan Szpakowicz. 2001. The design and implementation of an electronic lexical knowledge base. In *Proceedings the 14th Biennial Conference of the Canadian Society for Computational Studies of Intelligence (AI 2001*, pages 325–333.

Mario Jarmasz and Stan Szpakowicz. 2004. *Roget's Thesaurus* and semantic similarity. In Nicolas Nicolov, Kalina Bontcheva, Galia Angelova, and Ruslan Mitkov, editors, *Recent Advances in Natural Language Processing III. Selected papers from RANLP 2003*, pages 111–120. John Benjamins, Amsterdam.

Amanda C. Jobbins and Lindsay J. Evett. 1995. Automatic identification of cohesion in texts: Exploiting the lexical organization of Roget's Thesaurus. In *Proceedings of Rocling VIII*, pages 111–125, Taipei.

Amanda C. Jobbins and Lindsay J. Evett. 1998. Text segmentation using reiteration and collocation. In *Proceedings of the 36th ACL and 17th COLING, Volume 1*, pages 614–618, Montreal. ACL.

Richard Johansson and Luis Nieto Piña. 2015. Embedding a semantic network in a word space. In *Proceedings of the 2015 Conference of the North American Chapter of the Association for Computational Linguistics – Human Language Technologies*, Denver, United States. To appear.

Richard Johansson. 2014. Automatic expansion of the Swedish FrameNet lexicon. *Constructions and Frames*, 6(1):92–113.

Alistair Kennedy and Stan Szpakowicz. 2008. Evaluating *Roget's* thesauri. In *Proceedings of ACL-08: HLT*, pages 416–424, Columbus, Ohio. ACL.

Alistair Kennedy and Stan Szpakowicz. 2014. Evaluation of automatic updates of *Roget's Thesaurus*. *Journal of Language Modelling*, 2(2):1–49.

Adam Kilgarriff. 1997. I don't believe in word senses. *Computers and the Humanities*, 31(2):91–113.

Oi Yee Kwong. 1998. Aligning WordNet with additional lexical resources. In *Workshop on usage of WordNet in natural language processing systems at COLING-ACL'98*, pages 73–79, Montréal. ACL.

Lennart Lönngren. 1998. A Swedish associative thesaurus. In *Euralex '98 proceedings, Vol. 2*, pages 467–474.

Tomáš Mikolov, Kai Chen, Greg Corrado, and Jeffrey Dean. 2013. Efficient estimation of word representations in vector space. In *International Conference on Learning Representations, Workshop Track*, Scottsdale, USA.

Jane Morris and Graeme Hirst. 1991. Lexical cohesion computed by thesaural relations as an indicator of the structure of text. *Computational Linguistics*, 17(1):21–48.

M. Lynne Murphy. 2003. *Semantic relations and the lexicon*. Cambridge University Press, Cambridge.

Vivi Nastase and Stan Szpakowicz. 2001. Word-sense disambiguation in Roget's Thesaurus using WordNet. In *Workshop on WordNet and other lexical resources at NAACL*, Pittsburgh. ACL.

Roberto Navigli and Simone Paolo Ponzetto. 2012. BabelNet: The automatic construction, evaluation and application of a wide-coverage multilingual semantic network. *Artificial Intelligence*, 193:217–250.

Fabian Pedregosa, Gaël Varoquaux, Alexandre Gramfort, Vincent Michel, Bertrand Thirion, Olivier Grisel, Mathieu Blondel, Peter Prettenhofer, Ron Weiss, Vincent Dubourg, Jake VanderPlas, Alexandre Passos, David Cournapeau, Matthieu Brucher, Matthieu Perrot, and Edouard Duchesnay. 2011. Scikit-learn: Machine learning in Python. *Journal of Machine Learning Research*, 12:2825–2830.

Mark Peter Roget. 1852. *Thesaurus of English Words and Phrases*. Longman, London.

Peter D. Turney and Patrick Pantel. 2010. From frequency to meaning: Vector space models of semantics. *Journal of Artificial Intelligence Research*, 37:141–188.

Martine Vanhove, editor. 2008. *From polysemy to semantic change: Towards a typology of lexical semantic associations*. Jon Benjamins, Amsterdam.

Yorick Wilks. 1998. Language processing and the thesaurus. In *Proceedings National language Research Institute*, Tokyo. Also appeared as Technical report CS–97–13, University of Sheffield, Department of Computer Science.

Zhibiao Wu and Martha Palmer. 1994. Verb semantics and lexical selection. In *Proceedings of the 32nd Annual Meeting of the Association for Computational Linguistics*, pages 133–138, Las Cruces, New Mexico, USA.

Polysemy and questions of lumping or splitting in the construction of Swedish FrameNet

Karin Friberg Heppin
Språkbanken
Department of Swedish
University of Gothenburg
karin.friberg.heppin@svenska.gu.se

Dana Dannélls
Språkbanken
Department of Swedish
University of Gothenburg
dana.dannells@svenska.gu.se

Abstract

When working on a lexical resource, such as Swedish FrameNet (SweFN), assumptions based on linguistic theories are made, and methodological directions based upon them are taken. These directions often need to be revised when not beforehand foreseen problems arise. One assumption that was made already in the early development stages of SweFN was that each lexical entry from the reference lexicon, SALDO, would evoke only one semantic frame in SweFN. If a lexical entry evoked more than one frame, it entailed more than one sense and therefore required a new entry in the lexicon.

As work progressed, this inclination towards splitting, in the perpetual lumpers and splitters discussion (Kilgarriff, 1999), proved to be progressively untenable. This paper will give an account of the problems which were encountered and suggestions for solutions on polysemy issues forcing a discussion on lumping or splitting.

1 Introduction

Regular polysemy may be automatically recognized and disambiguated in a text if sufficient amount of data covering the word senses is provided (Alonso et al., 2013). For English, substantial computational work on automatic sense disambiguation has been done. Recent prominent work was carried out on **frame semantics** linguistic theory, more specifically Berkeley FrameNet (BFN) (Das et al., 2013). The vocabulary, comprising around 11,000 lexical units (LU), in BFN has been derived from annotated corpus sentences rather than from a lexicon. As a result, while less frequent words and word senses are represented, many frequently used word senses may be missing.

Furthermore, although BFN has a huge potential advantage for work on word sense disambiguation, it lacks formal definitions of polysemous behavior of words in frames. While there is, in many cases a straightforward relation between lexical units and semantic frames in BFN, there is no clear methodological approach for how to systematically deal with regular polysemy. Consequently, when building a new frame semantic resource, where BFN structure is taken as the interlingua, some theoretical and methodological approaches have to be considered.

In the construction of Swedish FrameNet, words with multiple semantically related meanings, i.e. polysemous Swedish lexical units, have forced more systematic approach to lumping or splitting of semantic frames and lexical entries.

In this paper we address problems of polysemy in FrameNet-like resources. We present polysemy problems we had to deal with during the construction of the frame semantics resource SweFN. We give an account of the reflections, and suggestions for solutions that have been taken on issues such as ambiguity, potential meaning, and vagueness, each forcing a discussion on lumping or splitting.

2 Swedish FrameNet (SweFN)

Swedish FrameNet has been developed as part of the SweFN++ project (Friberg Heppin and Toporowska Gronostaj, 2014; Borin et al., 2010) where the main objective is building a panchronic lexical macro-resource for use in Swedish language technology. This macro-resource consists of several separate resources with the SALDO lexicon (Borin et al., 2013) as the pivot resource to which all other resources are connected. One such resource is SweFN.

SweFN is a lexical semantic resource which has been constructed in line with Berkeley FrameNet

Karin Friberg Heppin and Dana Dannélls 2015. Polysemy, underspecification, and aspects – Questions of lumping or splitting in the construction of Swedish FrameNet. *Proceedings of the workshop on Semantic resources and semantic annotation for Natural Language Processing and the Digital Humanities at NODALIDA 2015.* NEALT Proceedings Series 27 / Linköping Electronic Conference Proceedings 112: 12–20.

(Ruppenhofer et al., 2010). The theoretical approach taken is based on frame semantics (Fillmore, 1982) which assumes that all content words in a language are best explained by appealing to the conceptual backgrounds that underlie their meanings. Word senses are described in relation to semantic frames, including the semantic roles of the participants.

We have transferred the conceptual layer of BFN to SweFN and provided one-to-one (in a few cases many-to-one) links to BFN frames. These frames were populated with language specific lexical units (LUs) derived from the lexicon SALDO, which evoke the frame in question, and example sentences from corpora. SweFN differs from BFN in several respects including a number of new frames unique to SweFN, compound analysis and domain information. As far as the methodological approach is concerned, the top-down frame building approach was extended with a bottom-up procedure, having its starting point in the lexicon, taking polysemous words and finding or creating frames for all regular (or systematic) senses (Apresjan, 1974). Disambiguation decisions were based on explicit lexical criteria and corpus-related data, to assure homogeneity and usefulness of the resulting resource.

To demonstrate the patterns of semantic roles, example sentences are added from the KORP corpus collection (Ahlberg et al., 2013). The KORP infrastructure offers a functionality called Word Picture which provides statistical information on lexical collocational features. When we add LUs to SweFN frames Word picture is used to acquire an overview of possible senses of Swedish nouns, verbs, and adjectives.

SALDO, Swedish Associative Thesaurus version 2, (Borin et al., 2013) is a free electronic lexicon resource for modern Swedish written language, containing around 130,000 lexical entries. It has an hierarchal structure where lexical entries are associated to each other through two semantic descriptors: primary and secondary. The primary descriptor is obligatory while the secondary one is optional. The resource can be compared to Princeton WordNet (Fellbaum, 1998) from which it differs in several aspects (Borin and Forsberg, 2009). On the polysemy level, the average degree of highly ambiguous words in SALDO is 4.7%, comparing to 12.4% in WordNet 3.1 (Johansson and Nieto Piña, 2015).

3 Cases of polysemy

According to BFN (Fillmore et al., 2003; Fillmore and Baker, 2009), if a word evokes more than one frame it is represented as different LUs with different senses. This is the background to the original stance of SweFN that each entry of the SALDO lexicon would only evoke one frame. Evoking a new frame entails a different sense and thus constitutes a different LU. In the work on SweFN we have encountered three types of cases where it, at first glance, would seem that a lexicon entry could evoke more than one frame: (1) two frames stand in a hyponomy relation to each other; (2) there is a regular polysemy relation between two frames; (3) the concept categories behind the frames divide the world along different dimensions. In the following we elaborate on each of these cases.

3.1 Hyponymy relation

When there is a hyponomy relation between frames we see two possible solutions: (1a) If a lexicon entry evokes more than one frame which all have a common parent frame, the entry becomes an LU evoking this parent frame. An example of this is the verb *bila* (car.v) 'go by car'. It may evoke both the `Operate_vehicle` and the `Ride_vehicle` frame. However, both these frames are in a hyponym relation to the `Use_vehicle` frame, and thus the LU *bila* is listed in this parent frame thereby evoking also the child frames which, i this case, are related to the parent frame in a Perspectivized relation (see Figure 1). (1b) If instead, a lexical entry evokes only one of several child frames in a hyponym relation to one common parent frame, the entry is listed as an LU in the child frame. In this case the LU may still evoke the parent frame. An example of this situation is found in the child frames `Medical_professionals`, `Member_of_military`, `Performers`, and `Representative`, all inheriting from the parent frame `People_by_vocation`.

3.2 Regular polysemy relation

For regular polysemy relation between two frames, case (2), it is difficult to avoid a certain degree of arbitrariness in decisions of when to lump and when to split, regardless of whether these decisions concern entries in the lexicon or frames in the framenet. Take as an example the relation between the `Food` and the `Animals` frames, and like-

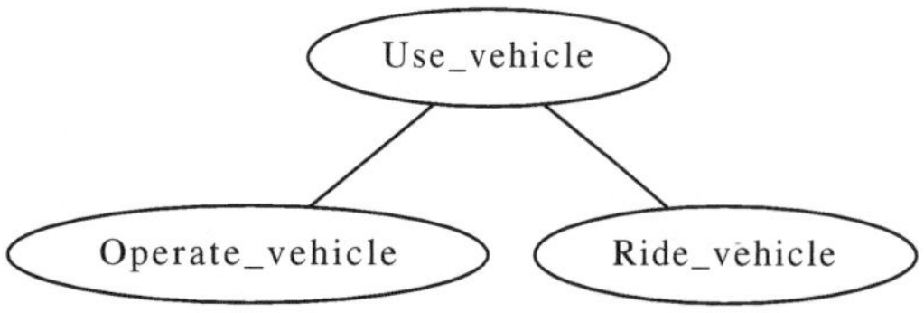

Figure 1: If a lexicon entry could evoke two frames which have a common frame in a hyperonym relation, as in the case with *bila* 'go by car', the entry is listed as an LU in the parent frame. Here `Use_vehicle` is perspectivized in both `Operate_vehicle` and `Ride_vehicle`.

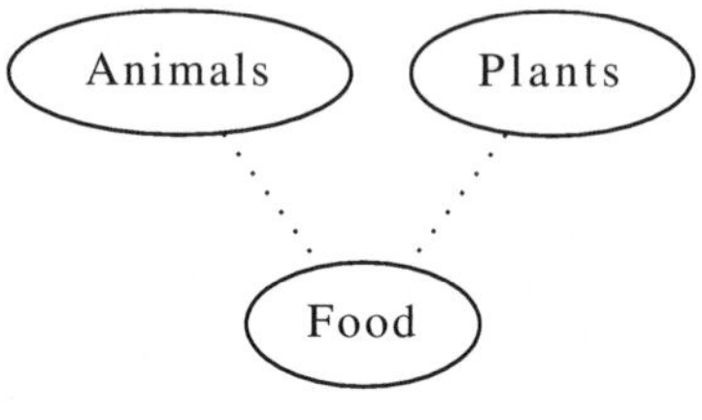

Figure 2: There is a regular polysemy relationship between `Animals` and `Plants` frames and the `Food` frame. All LUs in first frames could, with varying probability, evoke also the latter frame. In these cases they are Guest_LUs in this frame.

wise between the `Food` and the `Plants` frames. What constitutes food is matter from either animals or plants, the names of which become LUs evoking `Animals` or `Plants`. These words denoting animals or plants could also become LUs the `Food` frame, although with substantially varying probability, and in SweFN on the condition that they have separate entries in the SALDO lexicon. The probability that a certain word denoting animals or plants would have a food sense evoking the `Food` frame varies between cultures, circumstances of wellbeing, and what type of creature is doing the eating. In the SALDO lexicon there is only a small number of names of animals, e.g. *fisk* 'fish' and *lamm* 'lamb' with separate entries in the lexicon, for the animal and the food sense. Creating additional entries in the lexicon for additional animals and plants would not solve the problem as the decision on how probable in being consumed as food something would have to be in order to deserve a food sense in the lexicon would always be arbitrary. A solution to this situation, is to let LUs in the more basic frames, in this case `Animals` and `Plants`, appear as Guest_LUs in the other frame, as illustrated in Figure 2. A Guest_LU of a frame does not evoke this frame, and cannot be understood without the senses of the original frame, but may still, under certain circumstances evoke the frame in question. This means that example sentences may be given and annotated in the frame where the LU appears as Guest_LU (Ruppenhofer et al., 2010).

When there is a regular polysemy relation between frames it is not necessary to have more than one entry for a word in the lexicon or more than one LU evoking a frame in the framenet. However, from corpus evidence we learn that some species of animals and plants are more commonly consumed as food since they are considerably more frequent in the food sense than in other senses. Such evidence could for practical purposes make it meaningful to have additional entries in the lexicon. The entries, in turn, could be listed as LUs in the corresponding frame. For example, a corpus search on the word lax 'salmon' in Korp's Word Picture gives implicit hints for the most frequent senses of the word, as shown in Figure 3. The search resulted in 19,217 instances of *lax* from modern Swedish corpora. Almost all collocates of *lax* belong to the food sense: *färsk* 'fresh', *benfri* (bone-free) 'without bones', *med potatis* 'with potatoes', *i ugn* 'in oven', *äta* 'eat', *innehålla* 'contain', *servera* 'serve', and *laga* 'cook' Some collocates could go with either sense, such as *vara* 'be', *bli* 'become' and *köpa* 'buy'. Only three of the collocates belong exclusively to the animal sense, namely *fiska* 'fish', *fånga* 'catch', *rädda* 'rescue'. Even though results like the one descibed above may motivate additional lexicon entries, decisions of when to do so will always be arbitrary.

Many Swedish verbs show a tendency of construction shift in the object position. As a result, they evoke pairs of frames, for example, `Emptying` and `Removing`, e.g., *tömma* 'empty', *evakuera* 'evacuate', and `Placing` and `Filling`, e.g., *lasta* 'load'. Under the original assumption of SweFN this would entail different senses and consequently different entries in SALDO and listing as different LUs in the two frames. Examples 1 and 2 show such a construction shift which causes a shift of focus from what is being moved (THEME) to the original location (SOURCE). A problem with creating distinct entries in the lexicon is that these verbs frequently are used without lax (noun)

Preposition		Pre-modifier		Post-modifier	
1. med	929	1. färsk	303	1. med potatis	99
2. åt	74	2. norsk	173	2. i ugn	82
3. av	407	3. benfri	50	3. till middag	76
4. enligt	26	4. god	173	4. i bit	48
5. på	520	5. rå	44	5. i bit[2]	48
6. för	261	6. vild	48	6. i skiva	39
7. till	227	7. grav	31	7. med sås	32
8. ihop med	8	8. glad	57	8. med färskpotatis	22
9. över	25	9. 100g	19	9. med grönsaker	28
10. efter	54	10. 50g	12	10. med grönsak	28
11. i form	5	11. ekologisk	15		
12. utom	5	12. fin	32		
13. runt	10	13. smarrig	11		
14. efter smak	2	14. kall	18		
15. ovanpå	4	15. 400g	7		

Lax Verb		Verb lax	
1. äta	54	1. äta	474
2. vara	530	2. laga	181
3. bli	123	3. fiska	112
4. säga	54	4. köpa[2]	163
5. innehålla	34	5. köpa	163
6. servera	22	6. grilla	62
7. fånga	15	7. älska	84
8. fånga[2]	14	8. älska[2]	84
9. skära	13	9. fånga[2]	46
10. lägga	23	10. fånga	46
11. göra	42	11. göra	135
12. laga	13	12. servera	45
13. köpa[2]	21	13. käka	42
14. köpa	21	14. kosta	42
15. smaka	11	15. steka	32

Figure 3: A search for the noun *lax* 'salmon' in KORP's Word Picture tool shows that almost all collocates belong to the sense of *lax* evoking the `Food` frame. Only three, *vild* 'wild', *fånga* 'catch.v', and *fiska* 'fish.v' exclusively collocates with the sense evoking the `Animals` frame.

object, in which case, a specific sense is not expressed. This is a form of polysemy and the problem may be solved similarly to case (1), described in Section 3.2, by having only one sense in the lexicon, making this an LU evoking the most pertinent frame and letting it be a Guest_LU in the related frame. Polysemy due to construction change applies to many LUs in the concerned pairs of frames, but far from all LUs. Which frame is more pertinent also varies between LUs. This requires a specification on LU level for when the polysemy relation holds, and in which direction.

(1) Olov Lindgren hade redan evakuerat
Olof Lindgren had already evacuated
[många hyresgäster]THEME när [...]
many tenants when [...]
'Olof Lindgren had already evacuated many tenants when [...]' (`Removing`)

(2) [Byggnaden]SOURCE evakueras, [...]
'building-DEF evacuate-PASS
'The building is being evacuated [...]' (`Emptying`)

Other Swedish verbs with tendency to such construction changes evoke, among others, the `Removing-Emptying` frames, e.g., *tömma* 'empty' and *torka* 'wipe', and the `Placing-Filling` frames, e.g. *spreja* 'spray', *lasta* 'load'. A detailed description of corresponding construction changes for English may be found in Levin (2015) in the section on locative alternations.

3.3 Different dimensions

Finally, in the case of dividing the world into concepts along different dimensions, case (3), a solution may be to allow one lexical entry of the lexicon to evoke more than one frame. Consider the Swedish word for children who get one ear ache after the other: *öronbarn* (ear child) 'child that often gets ear aches'. As the sense is about persons being struck by disease, the LU evokes the frame `People_by_disease`. However, the word is used to denote children and therefore also evokes `People_by_age`, as in Example 3. This does not entail that there should be more than one entry in the lexicon, as both the age aspect and the disease aspect are evoked at the same time. What happens here is that the `People` frame is inherited by several frames dividing the concepts describing people along unrelated dimensions, e.g., `People_by_age` `People_by_disease` `People_by_morality` `People_by_vocation` etc. The consequense is that some lexical entries evoke more than one frame, especially in a language such as Swedish where compounding is a very productive linguistic process. The Danish WordNet has also dealt with this problem (Pedersen et al., 2010).

(3) I vår familj har vi öronbarn.
in our family have we ear-children.
'Our family's children often get ear aches'.

3.4 Complex relations

More than one of the situations, shown in cases (1)–(3) above, may be applicable for the some entries in the lexicon. A splitting approach, demanding one lexicon entry for each sense possibly evoking a frame, would in such cases result in a large number of lexicon entries, unmotivated from the perspective of how the words are used.

To illustrate this, consider the word *general* 'general'. The SALDO lexicon contains one entry for *general*, which now is listed in the SweFN `Member_of_military` frame. Other frames within the meaning potential would be `People_by_vocation`, `Leadership`, and `Appellations` (titles of individuals, often used together with the person's surname, e.g., *General Abas Khan*).

The current relations between frames in FrameNet show that `Member_of_military` inherits from `People_by_vocation`, a hyponomy relation described in case (1). The `Appellations` frame has a regular polysemy relation with `People_by_vocation` where all LUs in `People_by_vocation` could potentially evoke also the `Appellations` frame, regular polysemy relations described in case (2). At the same time the `Leadership` frame describes people along a different dimension than `People_by_vocation`, case (3). Being a leader may be inherent in being a general and a set of other vocations, but one does not need to have a profession or be in the military in order to be a leader. Neither is the case that all vocations or roles in the military involves being a leader. The sets of LUs evoking `Leadership` and `Member_of_military` or `People_by_vocation` are overlapping.

Summing it up, the SALDO entry *general* has several potential meanings which evoke the four frames `Member_of_military`, `People_by_vocation`, `Leadership`, and `Appellations`. Following the discussion above, the same lexical entry *general* would be listed in the `Member_of_military` and `Leadership` frames. As `Member_of_military` inherits from `People_by_vocation` *general* would also evoke `People_by_vocation`, and as there is a regular polysemy relation between this frame and `Appellations`, it would also evoke the latter frame as a Guest_LU. These relations are illustrated in Figure 4.

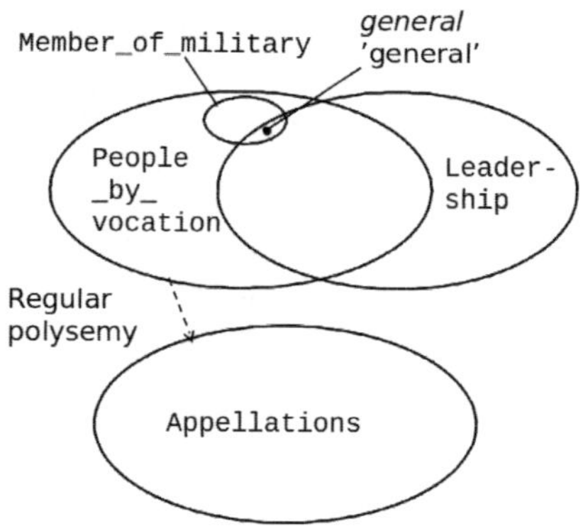

Figure 4: The lexical unit *general* evokes four frames without motivating as many entries in the lexicon. There is a hyponomy relation between the frames `People_by_vocation` and `Member_of_military`, an overlapping aspect of sense between these frames and the `Leadership` frame, while there is a regular polysemy relations between `People_by_vocation` (including `Member_of_military`) and the `Appellations` frames.

The cases described here in Section 3 show that the possibility of a lexicon entry evoking more than one frame does not always motivate adding a new sense to the lexicon or a regular LU to the framenet. In the current version of SweFN the lexical entries of SALDO are still only allowed to populate one frame. However, it has become obvious that solutions such as Guest_LU, additional parent frames, and allowing a lexicon entry to evoke more than one frame in restricted cases, must be considered.

4 Meaning potentials

The construction of a framenet tends to give bias to the splitting point of view. Work on a particular frame includes the phase of populating it with LUs. Encountering an entry in a lexicon, or a word/phrase in a corpus sentence, it is tempting to list it as an LU in the frame under construction if it in some sense evokes it. However, the potential of an entity to evoke a frame does not necessarily mean that this is the only frame it may evoke, or that it primarily evokes this frame. Hanks (2013) describes words as having **meaning potentials** in that different senses are activated in different contexts, something which does not entail that the word in question has several distinctive senses. This fuzzyness is not a flaw in language, but a strength, as it makes language dynamic and flexible, useful for describing situations and contexts never encountered before. Neither is it always desirable to be specific.

Even though frames evoked by the word's different meaning potentials may have varying semantic types, without explicit internal relation in, for example, the FrameNet system, many words still need to keep their vagueness and should have the possibility to evoke more than one frame. As stated by Wierzbicka (1984) the aim must sometimes be to be vague:

> An adequate definition of a vague concept must aim at precision in vagueness – it must aim at PRECISELY that level of vagueness which characterises the concept itself.(Wierzbicka, 1984):210

4.1 Diverse meaning potentials

A group of words which is often used underspecified, having several meaning potentials of diverse semantic types, are words denoting institutions/businesses/organizations, including the activities and people within. To illustrate this we can look at how the noun *skola* 'school' (in the education sense) is represented in *Svensk ordbok*, a monolingual Swedish dictionary published by the Swedish Academy (Allén et al., 2009):

- Institution where education is performed

1. with focus on the activities performed within the educational institution
2. with focus on the building where the education is performed
3. with focus on the collective of persons working with/attending educational activities within a certain institution
4. other organization which teaches a particular skill or subject

The noun has one main sense with four subsenses. The different subsenses could be said to evoke the frames in the list below. The list includes the initial part of the frame description in BFN:

- Main sense: `Institutions` "This frame concerns permanent organizations (the INSTITUTIONS) with a public character, meaning that they are intended to affect the lives of the public at large in a particular DOMAIN."
- Subsense 1: `Education_teaching` "This frame contains words referring to teaching and the participants in teaching."
- Subsense 2: `Buildings` "This frame contains words which name permanent fixed structures forming an enclosure and providing protection from the elements."
- Subsense 3: `Aggregate` "This frame contains nouns denoting AGGREGATES of INDIVIDUALS."
- Subsense 4: `Organization`. "This frame describes intentionally formed human social groups (here termed ORGANIZATIONS) with some definite structure and MEMBERS."

The various meaning potentials for a word are brought forward by the context, often put in focus by different collocates. Searching for collocates, with a tool such as Korp's Word Picture, may help detect senses, in a similar manner as for *lax* in Section 3.4. The collocational statistics for *school* in Word Picture shows that the main sense of the word together with subsenses 1 and 2 dominate.

Below is a list of frames followed by collocates to *skola* found by Word Picture. The frames are the ones which the potential meanings of *skola* evokes together with the collocates respectively:

- `Institutions`: *byta* 'change', *välja* 'choose', *driva* 'operate'
- `Education_teaching`: *kommunal* 'municipal', *vanlig* 'ordinary', *gå* 'attend'
- `Buildings`: *bygga* 'build', *ligga* 'be located', *brinna* 'be on fire'

The word *skola* shows several forms of regular polysemy in that is has several different meaning potentials, and is often used underspecified, including more than one sense. This is seen in Example 4 where the visitor, *Jag* 'I', may be seen as visiting the persons, the activities, as well as the building of the school itself. Making one entry in the lexicon for each potential, each becoming an LU evoking a different frame, would not catch the possibility of vagueness and the relations between the senses would be lost.

(4) Jag ska besöka en skola i Köpenhamn.
I will visit a school in Copenhagen.
'I am going to visit a school in Copenhagen.'

Words with the potential of denoting institutions, organizations, businesses, and the people and activities within, often show this type of regular polysemy, although with variying sets of potential meaning, and thus varying sets of frames evoked. In order to keep the possibility of vagueness between the potential meanings of varying semantic types, a system allowing Guest_LUs in the frames evoked by subsenses should be developed. However, as not all LUs in the basic frames, such as `Institutions`, `Businesses`, or `Organizations`, have the same set of subsenses, the Guest_LU relation must be established on the level of LUs, not frames.

The difficulty of choosing suitable frames for LUs denoting institutions, businesses, and organizations becomes apparent in the inconsistency in BFN for frames which are evoked by this group of nouns.

- *school* evokes `Locale_by_use`
- *theater* evokes `Buildings`, `Locale_by_use`, and `Fields`
- *bank* evokes `Businesses`
- *church* evokes `Buildings`
- *restaurant* evokes `Locale_by_use`
- *bar* evokes `Buildings`

Although there is a lack of consistency in how frames are split in BFN, BFN offers a possible solution for some cases of underspecification, the non-perspectivalized frame (Ruppenhofer et al., 2010). A frame of this type contains a diversity of LUs sharing a certain scene as background, but which do not have consistent semantic types. Examples are the `Education_teaching` frame, which is evoked by LUs such as *study*.v, *teach*.v, *training*.n, and *educational*.a and the `Performers_and_roles` frame evoked by, for example, *act*.v, *star*.n and *part*.n. To obtain consistent perspective in each frame, the frames could be split further, but then the possibility to house polysemous words would be lost.

However, the purpose of non-perspectivalized frames in BFN was not to house polysemous words, but is described as being as a time-saving measure (Ruppenhofer et al., 2010). The solution of having non-perspectivalized frames is not optimal in that having the definition of frames determined along the dimension of context instead of the dimension of participants and semantic roles, the frame definitions and division of the world are not consistent with each other.

4.2 Related meaning potentials

While some groups of words have diverse meaning potentials of a variety of semantic types, others have meaning potentials which are more closely related. Take the example of describing nationality or residence. There are words such as Canadian and Londoner which may describe persons with origin in a certain place. However, the same word may also describe where a person lives or where they are citizens. The origin of a person may well be different from were he or she resides or is registered. When stating a persons nationality or city it may be an advantage to be vague in this aspect.

In BFN and SweFN there are three frames which may be evoked by words for origin/residence/citizenship: `People_by_origin`, `Residence`, and `People_by_jurisdiction`, which inherit from the `People` frame.[1] Parts of the frame descriptions, from the FrameNet website,[2] are given below.

- `People_by_origin` – This frame contains words for individuals, i.e. humans, with respect to their ORIGIN.
- `Residence` – This frame has to do with people (the RESIDENTS) residing in LOCATIONS, sometimes with a CO-RESIDENT.
- `People_by_jurisdiction` – This frame contains words for individuals, i.e. humans,

[1] The `Residence` frame does not inherit directly from `People`, but stands in a 'Used by' relationship to the `People_by_residence` frame which, inherits from the `People` frame and in BFN contains the three LUs *housemate*, *neighbor*, and *roommate*.

[2] `https://framenet.icsi.berkeley.edu/fndrupal/`

who are governed by virtue of being registered in a certain JURISDICTION.

Most words denoting people in relation to geographic areas could evoke all of the frames above e.g., *stockholmare* (Stockholmer) 'person from Stockholm'. However, a few evoke only one e.g.: *malmöbo* (Malmö-liver) 'Malmö resident' evoking Residence, and *svenskfödd* (Swedish-born) 'born in Sweden' evoking (People_by_origin). For most of the words denoting people in relation to geographic areas it is desirable to maintain the possibility of vagueness, letting the context determine which meaning potentials should be realized. This may be solved by creating a new a frame on an intermediate level, inheriting from People and itself being inherited by the other three frames, with a name such as People_by_locale, for these LUs (see figure 5). The LUs which do not evoke all alternatives, such as *malmöbo* and *svenskfödd* should populate the frames that they do evoke. A solution such as this is a more elaborate example of case (1) described in Section 3.1.

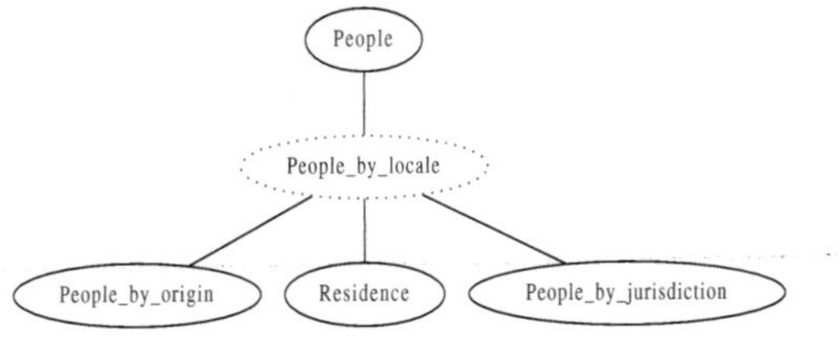

Figure 5: When meaning potentials evoke frames in close relation to each other, vagueness may be maintained by creating a new frame on an intermediate level, a parent frame to the more specific frames.

FrameNet has an intricate network of relations, such as inheritance or 'used by' relations between frames. For example, the frame People is inherited by several other frames, most of them with names on the format People_by_. A new frame, such as People_by_locale, would easily fit in this network having People as parent frame and the three frames described above as child frames. There are other cases where frames potentially evoked by an LU do not have connecting relations in the current FrameNet system, and are not as closely related. An example is the verb *bråka* 'fight', which may evoke both Quarreling inheriting from Discussion and Hostile_encounter inheriting from Intentionally_act and itself is inherited by Fighting_activity. Solving this, and similar cases which do not lend themselves easily into any case category, could be done, by consulting corpus data to see if any use is more frequent, or by looking at derivational forms related to the words in question. A *fighter*, for example, would more likely be involved in physical fights than quarrels, suggesting that the Hostile_encounter frame would be main frame evoked by *fight*, leaving *fight* to be a Guest_LU in Quarreling.

5 Summary

There are a number of situations where a lexical entry of the lexicon, here SALDO, evokes more than one frame in the framenet, here SweFN, but where it is still not motivated to split the entry into several polysemous entries. As the relations between the word senses and between the evoked frames differ, different cases must be treated in different ways. This does not necessarily constitute a problem in a resource such as BFN which is not directly linked to a specific lexicon. However, in the case of SweFN, where the original assumption was, and as far as possible still is, that each lexical entry of the SALDO lexicon should only evoke one frame, special account must be taken for entries with several senses potentially evoking different frames. This is especially the case when there is a restriction in that the resource must be compatible with other resources such as SweFN being part of the macro-resource SweFN++.

In cases of hyponymy relations between frames, where all child frames are evoked, it is sufficient to list the LUs in the parent frame. If not all child frames are evoked, the LUs should be listed in the child frames they do evoke. When there is a regular polysemy relation between frames, the lexical entries are listed as LUs in the most basic frame, and as Guest_LUs in the less basic frame. For some pairs of frames, the regular polysemy relation holds for all LUs, while for other frame pairs the relation might only concern a subset of these. This calls for a system of relations in the framenet, not only between frames, but also between LUs in pairs of frames.

Other situations where an LU evokes more than one frame is due to the manner FrameNet resources are constructed: pairs of frames may be overlapping, Leadership-People_by_vocation or frames may be non-perspectivalized such as

Education_teaching which is evoked by LUs of different semantic types within one domain. In these cases, the solution may be to allow, in a restricted manner, one lexicon sense become LU evoking more than one frame.

SweFN has had to let the assumption of one lexical entry – one frame be less restrictive. However, it is still the case that one SALDO entry cannot evoke more than one frame unless some type of relation is established. The exact forms of the relations are still to be decided.

Acknowledgments

We would like to thank Josef Ruppenhofer for his expert advise on FrameNet and Maria Toporowska Gronostaj for her expert advise in lexicography. The research presented here was supported by the Swedish Research Council (grant agreement 2010-6013), the Bank of Sweden Tercentenary Foundation (grant agreement P120076:1), and by the University of Gothenburg through its support of the Centre for Language Technology and of Språkbanken.

References

Malin Ahlberg, Lars Borin, Markus Forsberg, Martin Hammarstedt, Leif-Jöran Olsson, Olof Olsson, Johan Roxendal, and Jonatan Uppström. 2013. Korp and karp a bestiary of language resources: the research infrastructure of språkbanken. In *Proceedings of the 19th Nordic Conference of Computational Linguistics*, pages 429–433. NEALT.

Sture Allén, Daniel Berg, Sture Berg, Martin Gellerstam, Louise Holmer, Ann-Kristin Hult, Susanne Lindstrand, Sven Lövfors, Sven-Göran Malmgren, Christian Sjögreen, Emma Sköldberg, Lennart Tegner, and Maria Toporowska Gronostaj, editors. 2009. *Svensk ordbok utgiven av Svenska Akademien. 1-2.*

Héctor Martínez Alonso, Bolette Sandford Pedersen, and Núria Bel. 2013. Annotation of regular polysemy and underspecification. In *Proceedings from the 51st annual meeting in Association for Computational Linguistics*, pages 725–730. ACL.

J. Apresjan. 1974. Regular polysemy. *Linguistics*, 142:5–32.

Lars Borin and Markus Forsberg. 2009. All in the family: A comparison of SALDO and WordNet. In *Proceedings of the 17th Nordic Conference of Computational Linguistics (NODALIDA 2009)*, NEALT Proceedings Series, Vol. 4 (2009), Odense, Denmark. Kristiina Jokinen and Eckhard Bick.

Lars Borin, Dana Danélls, Markus Forsberg, Dimitrios Kokkinakis, and Maria Toporowska Gronostaj. 2010. The past meets the present in Swedish FrameNet++. In *14th EURALEX International Congress*, pages 269–281, Leeuwarden. EURALEX.

Lars Borin, Markus Forsberg, and Lennart Lönngren. 2013. SALDO: a touch of yin to WordNet's yang. *Language Resources and Evaluation*, 47(4):1191–1211.

Dipanjan Das, Desai Chen, André F. T. Martins, Nathan Schneider, and Noah A. Smith. 2013. Frame-Semantic Parsing. *Computational Linguistics*, 40(1):9–56.

Christiane Fellbaum. 1998. *WordNet: An electronic lexical database*. MIT Press.

Charles J. Fillmore and Collin Baker. 2009. A frames approach to semantic analysis. *The Oxford Handbook of Linguistic Analysis*, pages 313–340.

Charles J. Fillmore, Christopher R. Johnson, and Miriam R.L. Petruck. 2003. Background to FrameNet. *International Journal of Lexicography*, 16(3):235–250.

Charles J. Fillmore, 1982. *Frame semantics*, pages 111–137. Hanshin Publishing Co., Seoul, South Korea.

Karin Friberg Heppin and Maria Toporowska Gronostaj. 2014. Exploiting FrameNet for Swedish: Mismatch? *Constructions and Frames*, 6(1):52–72.

Patrick Hanks. 2013. *Lexical Analysis: Norms and Exploitations*. MIT Press, Cambridge, Mass.

Richard Johansson and Luis Nieto Piña. 2015. Combining relational and distributional knowledge for word sense disambiguation. In *Proceedings of the 20th Nordic Conference of Computational Linguistics*, Vilnius, Lithuania.

Adam Kilgarriff. 1999. I don't believe in word senses. *Computers and the Humanities*, 31(2):91–113.

Beth Levin. 2015. Semantics and pragmatics of argument alternations. *The Annual Review of Linguistics*, 1:63–83.

Bolette S. Pedersen, Sanni Nimb, and Anna Braasch. 2010. Merging specialist taxonomies and folk taxonomies in wordnets – A case study of plants, animals and foods in the Danish WordNet. In *Proc. of the Seventh International Conference on Language Resources and Evaluation*, Valletta, Malta. ELRA.

Josef Ruppenhofer, Michael Ellsworth, R. L. Miriam Petruck, R. Christopher Johnson, and Jan Scheffczy. 2010. *FrameNet II: Extended Theory and Practice*. ICSI, Berkeley.

Anna Wierzbicka. 1984. Cups and mugs: Lexicography and conceptual analysis. *Australian Journal of Linguistics*, 4(2):205–255.

Determining the Most Frequent Senses Using Russian Linguistic Ontology RuThes

Natalia Loukachevitch
Lomonosov Moscow State University
Moscow, Russia
louk_nat@mail.ru

Ilia Chetviorkin
Lomonosov Moscow State University
Moscow, Russia
Ilia2010@yandex.ru

Abstract

The paper describes a supervised approach for the detection of the most frequent senses of words on the basis of RuThes thesaurus, which is a large linguistic ontology for Russian. Due to the large number of monosemous multiword expressions and the set of RuThes relations it is possible to calculate several context features for ambiguous words and to study their contribution to a supervised model for detecting frequent senses.

1 Introduction

The most frequent sense (MFS) is a useful heuristic in lexical sense disambiguation when the training or context data are insufficient. In sense-disambiguation (WSD) evaluations the first sense labeling is presented as an important baseline (Agirre et al., 2007), which is difficult to overcome for many WSD systems (Navigli, 2009).

Usually MFS is calculated on the basis of a large sense-tagged corpus such as SemCor, which is labeled with WordNet senses (Landes et al., 1998). However, the creation of such corpora is a very labor-consuming task. Besides Princeton WordNet (Fellbaum, 1998), only for several other national wordnets such corpora are labeled (Perolito and Bond, 2014). In addition, the MFS of a given word may vary according to the domain, therefore the automatic processing of documents in a specific domain can require re-estimation of MFS on the domain-specific text collection. The distributions of lexical senses also can depend on time (Mitra et al., 2014).

Therefore automatic calculation of the most frequent sense is studied in several works (Mohammad and Hirst, 2006; McCarthy et al., 2004; McCarthy et al., 2007). One of the prominent approaches in this task is to use distributional vectors to compare contexts of an ambiguous word with sense-related words (Koeling et al., 2005; McCarthy et al., 2007). In such experiments mainly WordNet-like resources are studied. In (Mohammad, Hirst, 2006), the Macquarie Thesaurus serves as a basis for the predominant sense identification.

In this paper we present our experiments demonstrating how unambiguous multiword expressions can help to reveal the most frequent sense if they are allowed to be included in a thesaurus. The experiments are based on newly-published Thesaurus of Russian language RuThes-lite, which has been developed since 1994 and was applied in a number of tasks of natural language processing and information retrieval (Loukachevitch and Dobrov, 2014).

This paper is organized as follows. Section 2 compares our study with related works. In Section 3, we describe the main principles of RuThes-lite linguistic ontology construction. Section 4 is devoted to the manual analysis of the distribution of word senses described in RuThes, which is performed on the basis of Russian news flow provided by Yandex news service. Section 5 describes the experiments on supervised prediction of the most frequent sense of an ambiguous word.

2 Related Work

It was found in various studies that the most frequent sense is a strong baseline for many NLP tasks. For instance, only 5 systems of the 26 submitted to the Senseval-3 English all words task outperformed the reported 62.5% MFS baseline (Snyder and Palmer, 2004).

However, it is very difficult to create sense-labeled corpora to determine MFS, therefore techniques for automatic MFS revealing were proposed. McCarthy et al. (2004, 2007) describe

Natalia Loukachevitch and Ilia Chetviorkin 2015. Determining the most frequent senses using Russian linguistic ontology RuThes. *Proceedings of the workshop on Semantic resources and semantic annotation for Natural Language Processing and the Digital Humanities at NODALIDA 2015.* NEALT Proceedings Series 27 / Linköping Electronic Conference Proceedings 112: 21–27.

an automatic technique for ranking word senses on the basis of comparison of a given word with distributionally similar words. The distributional similarity is calculated using syntactic (or linear) contexts and the automatic thesaurus construction method described in (Lin, 1998). WordNet similarity measures are used to compare the word senses and distributional neighbors. McCarthy et al. (2007) report that 56.3% of noun SemCor MFS (random baseline – 32%), 45.6% verb MFS (random baseline – 27.1%) were correctly identified with the proposed technique.

In (Koeling et al., 2005) the problem of domain specific sense distributions is studied. They form samples of ambiguous words having a sense in one of two domains: SPORTS and FINANCE. To obtain the distribution of senses for chosen words, the random sentences mentioning the target words in domain-specific text collections are extracted and annotated.

Lau et al. (2014) propose to use topic models for identification of the predominant sense. They train a single topic model per target lemma. To compute the similarity between a sense and a topic, glosses are converted into a multinomial distribution over words, and then the Jensen – Shannon divergence between the multinomial distribution of the gloss and the topic is calculated.

Mohammad and Hirst (2006) describe an approach for acquiring predominant senses from corpora on the basis of the category information in the Macquarie Thesaurus.

A separate direction in WSD research is automatic extraction of contexts for ambiguous words based on so called "monosemous relatives" (Leacock et al., 1998; Agirre and Lacalle, 2004; Mihalcea 2002) that are related words having only a unique sense. It was supposed that extracted sentences mentioning monosemous relatives are useful for lexical disambiguation. These approaches at first determine monosemous related words for a given ambiguous word, then extract contexts where the relatives were mentioned, and use these contexts as automatically annotated data to train WSD classifiers.

In our case we use monosemous relatives in another way: to determine the most frequent senses of ambiguous words. We conduct our research for Russian and this is the first study on MFS prediction for Russian.

3 RuThes Linguistic Ontology

One of the popular resources used for natural language processing and information-retrieval applications is WordNet thesaurus (Fellbaum, 1998). Several WordNet-like projects were also initiated for Russian (Balkova et al., 2008; Azarowa, 2008; Braslavski et al. 2013). However, at present there is no large enough and qualitative Russian wordnet. But another large resource for natural language processing – RuThes thesaurus, having some other principles of its construction, has been created and published. The first publicly available version of RuThes (RuThes-lite) contains 96,800 unique words and expressions and is available from http://www.labinform.ru/ruthes/index.htm.

RuThes Thesaurus of Russian language is a linguistic ontology for natural language processing, i.e. an ontology, where the majority of concepts are introduced on the basis of actual language expressions. RuThes is a hierarchical network of concepts. Each concept has a name, relations with other concepts, a set of language expressions (words, phrases, terms) whose senses correspond to the concept, so called ontological synonyms.

Ontological synonyms of a concept can comprise words belonging to different parts of speech (*stabilization, stabilize, stabilized*); language expressions relating to different linguistic styles, genres; idioms and even free multiword expressions (for example, synonymous to single words).

So a row of ontological synonyms can include quite a large number of words and phrases. For instance, the concept *ДУШЕВНОЕ СТРАДАНИЕ* (*wound in the soul*) has more than 20 text entries (several English translations may be as follows: *wound, emotional wound, pain in the soul* etc.).

Besides, in RuThes introduction of concepts based on multiword expressions is not restricted and even encouraged if this concept adds some new information to knowledge described in RuThes. For example, a concept such as *ЗАСНУТЬ ЗА РУЛЕМ* (*falling asleep at the wheel)* is introduced because it denotes a specific important situation in road traffic, has an "interesting" text entry *заснуть во время движения* (*falling asleep while driving*). Also, this concept has an "interesting" relation to concept *ДОРОЖНО-ТРАНСПОРТНОЕ ПРОИСШЕСТВИЕ* (*road accident*) (Loukachevitch and Dobrov, 2014). The word "interesting" means here that the synonym and the relation do not follow from the component structure of phrase *заснуть за рулем*.

Thus, RuThes principles of construction give the possibility to introduce more multiword expressions in comparison with WordNet-like resources.

An ambiguous word is assigned to several concepts – this is the same approach as in WordNet. For example, the Russian word *картина (picture)* has 6 senses in RuThes and attributed to 6 concepts.

- *ФИЛЬМ* (*moving picture*)
- *ПРОИЗВЕДЕНИЕ ЖИВОПИСИ* (*piece of painting*)
- *КАРТИНА* (*ОПИСАНИЕ*) (*picture as description*)
- *КАРТИНА СПЕКТАКЛЯ* (*scene as a part of a play*)
- *ЗРЕЛИЩЕ (ВИД)* (*sight, view*)
- *КАРТИНА ПОЛОЖЕНИЯ, СОСТОЯНИЯ* (*picture as general circumstances*)

The relations in RuThes are only conceptual, not lexical (in contrast to antonyms or derivational links in wordnets). The main idea behind the RuThes set of conceptual relations is to describe the most essential, reliable relations of concepts, which are relevant to various contexts of concept mentioning. The set of conceptual relations includes the class-subclass relation, the part-whole relation, the external ontological dependence, and the symmetric association (Loukachevitch and Dobrov, 2014).

Thus, RuThes has considerable similarities with WordNet including concepts based on senses of real text units, representation of lexical senses, detailed coverage of word senses. At the same time, the differences include attribution of different parts of speech to the same concepts, formulating names of concepts, attention to multiword expressions, a set of conceptual relations. A more detailed description of RuThes and RuThes-based applications can be found in (Loukachevitch and Dobrov, 2014).

4 Manual Analysis of Sense Distribution

To check the coverage of lexical senses described in RuThes we decided to verify their usage in a text collection. At this moment we do not have the possibility to create a sense-tagged corpus based on RuThes senses. In addition, as it was indicated in (Petrolito and Bond, 2014), in sense-labeling most time and efforts are spent on adding new word senses to a source resource. Another problem of a sense-labeled corpus is that it fixes the described sets of senses, and it is impossible to automatically update them for a new version of a thesaurus.

To verify the coverage of lexical senses described in RuThes, the most important issue is to check that at least frequent senses have been already described. With this aim, it is not necessary to label all senses of a word in a large text collection, it is enough to check out senses in a randomly selected sample of word usages in contemporary texts as it was made in (Koeling, 2005). In addition, from this analysis we obtain manual estimation of MFS.

We decided to check RuThes senses on news texts and articles through Yandex news service[1]. We based our evaluation on a news collection because news reports and articles are one of the most popular documents for natural language processing, such as categorization, clustering, information extraction, sentiment analysis. Besides, the news collection comprises a lot of other text genres as legal regulations or literature pieces. Finally, this collection contains recently appeared senses, which can be absent in any fixed collection such as, for example, Russian national corpus (Grishina and Rakhilina, 2005) and dictionaries.

Yandex.news service collects news from more than 4,000 sources (including main Russian Newspapers), receiving more than 100,000 news articles during a day. The news flow from different sources is automatically clustered into sets of similar news. When searching in the service, retrieval results are also clustered. Usually three sentences from the cluster documents (snippets) are shown to the user.

For a given ambiguous word, linguists analyzed snippets in Yandex news service, which returns the most recent news reports and newspaper articles containing the word. Considering several dozens of different usages of the word in news, the linguists estimated the distribution of senses of the word, which later would allow defining the most frequent sense of the word. In news snippets, repetitions of the

[1] http://news.yandex.ru/

same sentences can be frequently met – such repetitions were dismissed from the analysis. Table 1 presents the results of the analysis for Russian ambiguous words *провести (provesti), картина (kartina),* and *стрелка (strelka).* The sense distributions for these three words have quite different behavior. Word *провести* has a single predominant sense; word *картина* has two main senses with approximately similar frequencies. Word *стрелка* has three enough frequent senses.

Because of insufficient amount of data under consideration, the experts could designate several senses as the most frequent ones if they saw that the difference in the frequencies does not allow them to decide what a sense is more frequent. For example, for word *картина* two main senses were revealed: *ФИЛЬМ (moving picture)* and *ПРОИЗВЕДЕНИЕ ЖИВОПИСИ (piece of painting)* (Table 1).

Word	Name of concept corresponding to senses of the word	Number of contexts
Провести (provesti) 9 senses	*ПРОВЕСТИ, ОРГАНИЗОВАТЬ, УСТРОИТЬ* (organize)	19
	ПРОЛОЖИТЬ ЛИНИЮ, ПУТЬ (build road, pipe)	1
Картина (kartina) 6 senses	*ПРОИЗВЕДЕНИЕ ЖИВОПИСИ* (piece of painting)	10
	ФИЛЬМ (moving picture)	10
Стрелка (strelka) 7 senses	*СТРЕЛКА РЕК* (river spit)	8
	СТРЕЛКА ПРИБОРА (pointer of the device)	6
	ЗНАК СТРЕЛКИ (arrow sign)	4
	ЖЕЛЕЗНОДОРОЖ-НАЯ СТРЕЛКА (railroad point)	1
	СТРЕЛКА НА ЧАСАХ (clock hand)	1

Table 1. Sense distribution of several Russian ambiguous words in the news flow (20 different contexts in current news flow were analyzed)

In total, around 3,000 ambiguous words with three or more senses described in RuThes (11,450 senses altogether) were analyzed in such a manner. As a result of such work, about 650 senses (5.7%) were added or corrected. So the coverage of senses in RuThes was enough qualitative and improved after the analysis.

Certainly, the distribution of word senses in news service search results can be quite dependent on the current news flow; in addition, the subjectivity of individual expertise can appear. Therefore for 400 words the secondary labeling was implemented, which allows us to estimate inter-annotator (and inter-time) agreement. 200 words from these words had three senses described in RuThes, other 200 words had four and more described senses.

The table 2 demonstrates that for 88% of the words, experts agreed or partially agreed on MFS for the analyzed words (Kappa=0.83). The partial agreement means in this case that experts agreed on prominent frequency of at least one sense of a word and indicated other different senses as also prominent. For example, for word *картина,* the first expert indicated two main senses (*moving picture* and *piece of painting*) with equal frequencies. The second expert revealed that the *piece of painting* sense is much more frequent than other senses. Therefore we have here partial agreement between experts and suppose that the most frequent sense of a word is the *piece of painting* sense.

Number of words analyzed by two experts	400
Number of words for that experts agreed on MFS	216
Number of words for that experts partially agreed on MFS	125
Number of words for that experts did not agreed on MFS	49

Table 2. The agreement in manual estimation of the most frequent senses for ambiguous words described in RuThes.

5 Supervised Estimation of Most Frequent Sense

The described in the previous section expert annotation of the most frequent senses was performed only for ambiguous words with three or more senses described in RuThes. Besides, RuThes contains about 6,500 words with two senses, which were not analyzed manually. In addition, MFS can vary in different domains; natural language processing of documents in a specific domain can require re-estimation of MFS on the domain collection.

Therefore we propose a method for supervised estimation of MFS based on several features calculated on the basis of a target text collection. To our knowledge, this is the first attempt to apply a supervised approach to MFS estimation. In addition, in contrast to previous works our method of MFS estimation is essentially based on unambiguous text entries of RuThes, especially on multiword expressions, which were carefully collected from many sources.

The automatic estimation of the most frequent sense was performed on a news collection of two million documents. Computing features for the supervised method we used several context types of a word: *the same sentence context, the neighbor sentence context, full document context.*

From the thesaurus, we utilize several types of conceptual contexts of an ambiguous word *w*:

- one-step context of word *w* attached to concept *C* ($ThesCon_{w1}$) that comprises other words and expressions attached to the same concept C and concepts directly related to C as described in the thesaurus;
- two and three-step contexts of word *w* attached to C ($ThesCon_{w2(3)}$) comprising words and expressions from the concepts located at the distance of maximum 2 (3) relations to the initial concept C (including C); the path between concepts can consist of relations of any types,
- one-step thesaurus context including only unambiguous words and expressions: $UniThesCon_{w1}$.

From these text and thesaurus contexts we generate the following features for ambiguous word *w* and its senses C_w:

- the overall collection frequency of expressions from $UniThesCon_{w1}$ – here we estimate how often unambiguous relatives of *w* were met in the collection – $Freqdoc_1$ and logarithm of this value *logFreqdoc*, Table 3 depicts frequencies of monosemous relatives of word *картина* in the source collection,
- the frequency of expressions from $UniThesCon_{w1}$ in texts where *w* was mentioned – $FreqdocW_1$,
- the overall frequency and the maximum frequency of words and expressions from $ThesCon_{wi}$ co-occurred with *w* in the same sentences – $FreqSentWmax_i$ and $FreqSentWsum_i$ (i=1, 2, 3),
- the overall frequency and the maximum frequency of words and expressions from $ThesCon_{wi}$ occurred in the neighbor sentences with *w* – $FreqNearWmax_i$ and $FreqNearWsum_i$ ((i=1, 2, 3).

All real-valued features are normalized by dividing them by their maximal value.frequency

Monosemous relatives of word *картина*	sense of *картина*	document
Фильм (film)	*moving picture*	45285
мультфильм (cartoon)	*moving picture*	4097
документальный фильм (documentary film)	*moving picture*	3516
живопись (painting)	*piece of painting*	3200
съемка фильма (shooting a film)	*moving picture*	2445
кинофильм (movie)	*moving picture*	1955
произведение искусства (art work)	*piece of painting*	1850
художественный фильм (fiction movie)	*moving picture*	1391
изобразительное искусство (visual art)	*piece of painting*	1102
режиссер картины (director of the movie)	*moving picture*	978
общая картина (general picture)	*general circums-tances*	932

Table 3. Document frequencies of monosemous relatives of word *картина* in the source collection of 2 mln. documents

We conduct our experiments on two sets of ambiguous words with three or more senses. The first set (*Set1*) consists of 330 words of 400 words that were analyzed by two linguists. They agreed with each other on one or two the most frequent senses. We used this set to train machine learning models. We apply the trained model to the second set of ambiguous words – 2532 words (*Set2*), for which only one expert provided MFS. Both sets include words of three parts of speech: nouns, verbs and adjectives.

The Table 4 presents accuracy results of MFS detection for single features. One can see that many single features provide a quite high level of accuracy.

Feature	Accuracy
$Freqdoc_1$	42.4%
$FreqdocW_1$	46.4%
$FreqSentWsum_1$	41.2%
$FreqSentWmax_1$	43.3%
$FreqSentWsum_2$	**48.2%**
$FreqSentWmax_2$	**48.2%**
$FreqSentWsum_3$	47.0%
$FreqSentWmax_3$	47.6%
$FreqNearWsum_1$	43.0%
$FreqNearWmax_1$	44.2%
$FreqNearWsum_2$	39.7%
$FreqNearWmax_2$	46.7%
$FreqNearWsum_3$	38.8%
$FreqNearWmax_3$	43.3%
Supervised algorithm	**50.6%**
Random	23.5%

Table 4. Accuracy of MFS prediction for single features and the supervised algorithm for Set1

To combine the features regression-oriented methods implemented in WEKA machine learning package were utilized. The best quality of classification using labelled data was shown by the ensemble of three classifiers: Logistic Regression, LogitBoost and Random Forest. Every classifier ranged word senses according to probability of this sense to be the most frequent one. We averaged probabilities of MFS generated by these methods. We obtained 50.6% accuracy of MFS prediction, the random baseline for this set is very low – 23.5% (Table 4). Our estimation is based on ten-fold cross validation.

To check the robustness of the obtained supervised model we applied it to the Set2. Table 5 describes the accuracy results for the best single features and the supervised method. The average level of results is higher than on the Set1, because Set2 contains the larger share of 3-sense words.

Feature	Accuracy
$FreqSentWsum_1$	53.7%
$FreqSentWsum_2$	**57.4%**
$FreqSentWmax_2$	53.7%
$FreqSentWsum_3$	54.6%
$FreqNearWsum_2$	53.7%
Supervised algorithm trained on Set1	**57.8%**
Random	33.4%

Table 5. Accuracy of MFS prediction for words from Set2 including accuracy of the best single features and accuracy of the supervised algorithm trained on Set1

We can see that simple context features give the accuracy results comparable with those described in (McCarthy et al., 2004; McCarthy et al., 2007), which have similar levels of random baselines (see Section 2). At this moment machine-learning combination of features did not demonstrate the significant growth in accuracy but the machine-learning framework allows adding distributional features utilized in the above-mentioned works.

6 Conclusion

In this paper we describe a supervised approach to detecting the most frequent senses of ambiguous words on the basis of thesaurus of Russian language RuThes. The approach is based on monosemous relatives of ambiguous words, in particular multiword expressions, described in RuThes. To check the proposed approach two linguists manually estimated the most frequent senses for 3,000 ambiguous words described in RuThes with three or more senses.

Our approach demonstrates its quality, which is quite comparable to the state-of-art distributional approaches, but our approach is based on simpler context features.

We found that some simple features (such as frequency of 2-step monosemous relatives of a word in sentences with this word – $FreqSentWsum_2$) provide high level of prediction of the most frequent sense.

We believe that in combination with other distributional features of words proposed in previous works it is possible to achieve better results in future experiments on MFS prediction.

Acknowledgments

This work is partially supported by Russian Foundation for Humanities grant N15-04-12017.

References

Eneko Agirre, and Oier Lopez De Lacalle. 2004. Publicly Available Topic Signatures for all WordNet Nominal Senses. *Proceedings of LREC-2004.*

Eneko Agirre, Lluís Màrquez, and Richard Wicentowski., Eds. 2007. *Proceedings of the 4th International Workshop on Semantic Evaluations* (SemEval). Association for Computational Linguistics, Prague, Czech Republic.

Irina Azarowa. 2008. RussNet as a Computer Lexicon for Russian. *Proceedings of the Intelligent Information systems IIS-2008*: 341-350.

Valentina Balkova, Andrey Suhonogov, and Sergey Yablonsky. 2008. Some Issues in the Construction of a Russian WordNet Grid. *Proceedings of the Forth International WordNet Conference*, Szeged, Hungary: 44-55.

Pavel Braslavski, Dmitrii Ustalov, and Mikhail Mukhin. 2014. A Spinning Wheel for YARN: User Interface for a Crowdsourced Thesaurus. *Proceedings of EACL-2014*, Sweden.

Christiane Fellbaum. 1998. *WordNet: An Electronic Lexical Database.* Cambridge, MA: MIT Press.

Elena Grishina, and Ekaterina Rakhilina. 2005. Russian National Corpus (RNC): an overview and perspectives. *AATSEEL- 2005.*

Rob Koeling, Diana McCarthy, and John Carroll. 2005. Domain-specific sense distributions and predominant sense acquisition. *Proceedings EMNLP-2005*, Vancouver, B.C., Canada: 419-426.

Shari Landes, Claudia Leacock, and Randee Tengi. 1998. Building semantic concordances. *In Fellbaum, C. (ed.) WordNet: An Electronic Lexical Database*. Cambridge (Mass.): The MIT Press.

Jey Han Lau, Paul Cook, Diana McCarthy, Spandana Gella, and Timothy Baldwin. 2014. Learning Word Sense distributions, Detecting Unattested Senses

Word Sense Disambiguating Systems: 41-43.

Tommaso Petrolito and Francis Bond. 2014. A Survey of WordNet Annotated Corpora. *In Proceedings Global WordNet Conference, GWC-2014*: 236-245.

and Identifying Novel Senses Using Topic Models.

Extraction of Lethal Events from Wikipedia and a Semantic Repository

Magnus Norrby
Lund University
Department of Computer Science
221 00 Lund, Sweden
mange.norrby@gmail.com

Pierre Nugues
Lund University
Department of Computer Science
221 00 Lund, Sweden
Pierre.Nugues@cs.lth.se

Abstract

This paper describes the extraction of information on lethal events from the Swedish version of Wikipedia. The information searched includes the persons' cause of death, origin, and profession. We carried out the extraction using a processing pipeline of available tools for Swedish including a part-of-speech tagger, a dependency parser, and manually-written extraction rules. We also extracted structured semantic data from the Wikidata store that we combined with the information retrieved from Wikipedia. Eventually, we gathered a database of facts that covers both sources: Wikipedia and Wikidata.

1 Introduction

Wikipedia contains a large number of biographies in many languages, where key events in the life of a person are described in plain text. As a complement to the Wikipedia narrative, Wikidata is a data repository that assigns Wikipedia entities unique identifiers across languages: A sort of social security number valid across all the Wikipedia territories.

Wikidata was primarily designed to ease the interconnection between multilingual web pages, but it now links entities with a growing number of semantic properties, such as for a person, a birth name (P1477), sex or gender (P21), etc.; for an administrative territorial entity (country), a capital (P36), a currency (P38), an official language (P37), etc. For instance, the entity *Jimi Hendrix* has the unique identifier Q5928 with properties such his date of birth, *27 November 1942*, and of death (P570): *18 September 1970*. The relatively language-agnostic structure of Wikidata makes it a very convenient semantic resource that can potentially be applied with no adaptation to any language version of Wikipedia.

This article explores means to extract information about lethal events from texts including the date and cause of death of people, using a relatively simple text processing architecture consisting of a part-of-speech tagger and a dependency parser and this large, language-independent, graph-oriented semantic repository.

We gathered the texts from the Swedish Wikipedia and the extracted data was then compared with data found in Wikidata. We stored the resulting extracted information in an SQL database. The collected data could then easily be queried to answer questions about the population on Wikipedia. A question we had in mind when we evaluated our database was how to answer the puzzling and much-debated coincidence:

> Do all the legendary musicians die at 27?

2 Previous Work

The work we describe in this paper is an information extraction task using the Swedish version of Wikipedia, Wikipedia categories, and a rich semantically annotated data set: Wikidata.

Information extraction systems are now ubiquitous and there are countless references that describe them. The Message Understanding Conferences (MUC) standardized their evaluation and the pipeline architecture eloquently advocated by the FASTUS system (Appelt et al., 1993; Hobbs et al., 1997) is still followed by scores of information extraction systems.

Many information extraction systems use now

Magnus Norrby and Pierre Nugues 2015. Extraction of lethal events from Wikipedia and a semantic repository. *Proceedings of the workshop on Semantic resources and semantic annotation for Natural Language Processing and the Digital Humanities at NODALIDA 2015.* NEALT Proceedings Series 27 / Linköping Electronic Conference Proceedings 112: 28–35.

the Wikipedia collection of articles as a source of information as it is freely available and, although disputed, of relatively good quality. It also provides semi-structured data which can complement the text.

Wu and Weld (2007) is an example of it, where the authors designed a system to extract values of predefined properties from the article text and complement infoboxes or to improve document categorization.

Lange et al. (2010) parsed the Wikipedia running text to extract data and populate the article's infoboxes. Their strategy is more complex than the one described in this paper since they handled more than 3,000 Wikipedia different template structures. In our case, we always looked for the same type of data and could therefore in many cases find the needed information in the page categories, instead of the free text.

Chernov et al. (2006) is another project that used the semantic information between the category links in an attempt to improve Wikipedia's search capabilities.

In this paper, we combined Wikipedia, the relatively new Wikidata semantic repository, and language-processing components for Swedish to extract information and store it in a fashion that is easier to search.

3 Dataset

We chose the Swedish Wikipedia as initial dataset that we downloaded from the Wikipedia dump pages. The dump consists of a compressed XML tree that we parsed with the Bliki XML Parser (Bliki, 2014) to produce HTML pages. We then used Sweble's Wikitext Parser (Dohrn and Riehle, 2013) to reduce the articles from HTML to raw text. From this corpus, we extracted a set of persons, their place of origin, their professions, dates of birth and death, place of death, and finally the cause of their death.

4 Wikipedia Categories

We first extracted a set of human entities from the whole collection. To carry this out, we used the Wikipedia category: *birth by year* "Födda" (`Category:Births_by_year`) that lists persons by their year of birth followed by the word *births*, i.e. "1967 births". A similar category lists persons by their year of death: *deaths by year* "Avlidna" (`Category:Deaths_by_year`), for instance "1994 deaths".

The latter category allowed us to narrow the search from all the persons to persons who passed away and thus where the pages possibly contained a lethal event. We applied regular expressions on the raw text to find these categories. We parsed all pages and we saved the pages where we found both categories. This way, we collected a dataset of 78,151 Swedish Wikipedia pages, all describing persons.

5 Extraction from Text

For each page, the Bliki XML Parser extracts both the page title, here a person's name, and the Wikipedia numeric page ID. If two persons have the same name, Wikipedia adds more information to make the title unique. For example, the Swedish Wikipedia lists nine different Magnus Nilsson. These pages are given titles like *Magnus Nilsson (kung)* "Magnus Nilsson (king)", *Magnus Nilsson (född 1983)* "Magnus Nilsson (born 1983)", etc. The added information is always contained within two parentheses and we extracted the name by splitting the string at the "(" character. To maintain a unique ID for each person when the names could be identical, we used the numeric page ID instead.

5.1 Parsing the Text

We built a processing pipeline consisting of a part-of-speech (POS) tagger and a dependency parser that we applied to the documents.

We first tagged all the documents with the Stagger POS tagger for Swedish (Östling, 2013). We then applied the MaltParser dependency parser (Nivre et al., 2006) on the tagged sentences.

We saved the results in a CoNLL-like format consisting of the following columns: token counter (ID), form, lemma, coarse POS tag, POS tag, grammatical features, head, and dependency relation. In addition, Stagger output named entity tags that supplement the CoNLL columns.

5.2 Date Extraction

We extracted the dates from their POS tags. A date like *11 January 1111* is tagged as RG NN RG, where RG represents a base number and NN, a noun. We searched this specific pattern in all the sentences and we checked that the noun belonged to one of the twelve months using string matching.

We cross-checked these dates with the categories from Sect. 4 corresponding to the year of birth and the year of death and we saved them when they agreed.

This method could certainly be improved as it does not take into account that these dates could describe other events. To reduce the risk of saving a wrong date, we compared them internally. If more than one date was found on the same birth year, we chose the earliest and we applied the reverse for death years. This assumes that all dates referred to dates while the person was alive which, of course, is a simplification.

5.3 Extraction from Categories

The categories of Wikipedia pages are simple phrases that state facts about the page such as the person's profession or cause of death. The key difference between the page categories and free text is that the categories have a specific pattern and connect other pages with the same categories. This means that we can add common categories that describe information we want to extract to our search pattern.

Since the page categories are created and added by users, the categorization sometimes contains mistakes, while some information is omitted. A page describing a guitarist might lack the category *Guitarists* but contain the tag *Left-handed guitarists*. This means that we cannot solely depend on the string matching, but also apply our tagger to the categories. Fortunately as noted by Nastase and Strube (2008), the analysis of these short phrases are much easier than for free text or even simple sentences.

5.3.1 Causes of Death

We extracted the causes of death from the page categories. We collected manually these categories through the examination of Wikipedia pages. We then used string matching to extract the causes of death of all the persons we had in our collection.

Although relatively consistent, same kinds of events can be assigned different categories. Assassinations and murders commonly use the category *Personer som blivit mördade* in Swedish, literally *Persons that have been murdered*, that corresponds to the English category *Murder victims*. However, Martin Luther King is assigned another category instead: *Mördade amerikanska politiker* equivalent to *Assassinated American politicians* in English. The string patterns used to extract the causes of death are shown below while Table 1 shows their equivalent categories in the English Wikipedia.

- *Personer som blivit mördade*, English Wikipedia: *Murder victims* "Persons that have been murdered"
- *Mördade* "Murdered"
- *Personer som begått självmord* "Suicides"
- *Personer som drunknat* "Persons that have drowned"
- *Personer som blivit avrättade* "Persons that have been executed"
- *Personer som avrättades* "Persons that were executed"
- *Personer som stupat i strid* "Persons who died in battle"

Swedish category	Equivalent English category
Personer som blivit mördade	Murder victims
Personer som begått självmord	Suicides
Personer som drunknat	Deaths by drowning
Personer som blivit avrättade	Executed people
Personer som stupat i strid	Military personnel killed in action

Table 1: English equivalent to categories used to extract the causes of death.

Some categories were not as straightforward as with the phrase *Personer som dött av...* "Persons who died of..." that appeared in many different categories such as *Personer som dött av idrottsolyckor* "Persons who died of sport injuries". Since we knew that the categories only contained one sentence we could just strip the part *Personer som dött av* and we saved the remainder as the cause.

5.3.2 Places of Origin

We limited the places of origin to be either a country, a town, or another geographical region. A person was allowed to have multiple origins and we did not make a difference between the different origin types. Because of the recurring syntax of the categories, we used simple patterns. The first approach was to find categories containing the string *från* "from". This method captured all the categories with the syntax *Person från ORIGIN* "Person from ORIGIN".

We used the strings *Musiker i* "Musicians in" as with *Musiker i Sverige under 1600-talet* "Musicians in Sweden during the 15th century". We chose these strings because they are relatively frequent in the Swedish Wikipedia. We used a similar approach with categories containing the string *Personer i* "Persons in" to match the pattern *Personer i ORIGIN TAIL*, where the tail could be anything.

This method found a lot of false positives as for instance *Personer i grekisk mytologi* "Persons in Greek mythology". Most of the false positives could be removed by checking if the word marked as origin began with a capital letter. However, this approach would not work well in English as can be seen in the example above.

5.4 Extractions using Dependency Parsing

In addition to the patterns applied to the categories, we analyzed the dependency parse trees from the text to extract further information.

5.4.1 Places of Origin

To complement the places of origin obtained from the categories, we searched for paths in the trees linking the name of the person to a word tagged as a place by Stagger. These paths had to go through the verb *föda* "bear", or its inflections. We added the relations we found to the database.

5.4.2 Details on the Death

To add details on the death, we searched the words *dödsorsak* "cause of death" or *avled* "passed away" and we examined their modifiers. Causes of death often involved the grammatical function tag PA corresponding to the complement of preposition. We used this function in combination with a noun (NN) to detect the cause. We applied additional rules to capture the specifics of the whole cause. If for instance, the word after the identified cause was *på* "on" that word and the word after was also added to the cause. This made sure that we handled causes like *ruptur på aortan* "Aortic aneurysm" correctly.

6 Extraction from a Semantic Repository

6.1 Wikidata

Wikidata is a database of Wikipedia entities. It started as a means to provide a better linking mechanism between the different language versions of the Wikipedia pages. Each entity was assigned a unique identifier in the form of a Q-number. For instance, the Swedish writer Astrid Lindgren has the number Q55767, Gustave Flaubert has the number Q43444, and Denmark has the number: Q35.

Entities with the same name as Casablanca receive different numbers: Q7903 for the Moroccan city and Q132689 for the American movie. Using the address: http://www.Wikidata.org/wiki/Q55767, it is possible to access all the versions of the Astrid Lindgren pages: 72 pages in total.

In addition to the unique number identification, Wikidata links the entity to properties, for instance a sex and gender, P21, a place of birth, P19, a country of citizenship, P27, a supercategory (instance of), P31, etc. For Astrid Lindgren, the corresponding key-value pairs are:

- P21 = female (Q6581072)
- P19 = Vimmerby (Q634231)
- P27 = Sweden (Q34)
- P31 = human (Q5)
- etc.

There are now hundreds of properties that are stored in the form of RDF triples and the list is growing.

As with Wikipedia, we parsed Wikidata with the Bliki XML parser and we stored the results in the JSON format.

6.2 Identifying Persons

We parsed all the Wikidata pages to identify persons using the JSON Simple parser (Fang, 2012). We extracted them by considering the property *instance of*, P31, and the value *human* (Q5).

We did not try to find new persons, but only to add information to persons already identified from Wikipedia. The next step was therefore to find the name of the person described and see if it matched any name we already had. This was done by looking at the JSON entity labels. If it contained the entity "sv", which marked the existence of a Swedish page, we saved its value as a string. If that string matched any of our saved persons name from Wikipedia, we defined them as the same person and continued to parse the page.

6.3 Extraction

The extraction was fairly straightforward from of the Wikidata properties. We used:

- Place of birth (P19)
- Place of death (P20)
- Occupation (P106)
- Cause of death (P509)
- Date of birth (P569)
- Date of death (P570)
- Manner of death (P1196)

Wikidata makes a difference between *cause of death* and *manner of death*, which we did not do while searching Wikipedia. If we found both for a person, we used the manner of death.

We merged these properties with those we extracted from Wikipedia.

7 Combining Results

Table 2 shows the number of extractions from the Wikipedia text and from Wikidata, where the combined column is the combination of unique values. Table 3 shows the number of unique and shared values.

We can assume that we retrieved all the data available from Wikidata. This gives us an idea of the accuracy of the Wikipedia extractions. As the tables show, we found very few causes of death. The numbers might look pretty weak at a first glance but when they are compared to Wikidata, we see that the information was very rarely present.

The data set coming from Wikidata is smaller since we only accepted persons that we could link to those previously extracted from Wikipedia. This means that we cannot directly compare the absolute values from Wikidata and Wikipedia. Table 4 shows the extraction rates compared to the data set size.

If we use Wikidata as a baseline, we can see that our Wikipedia extractions performs well in both

	Wikipedia	Wikidata	Both
Persons	78,151	61,410	78,151
Origins	47,174	36,268	75,341
Professions	95,792	69,429	140,654
Place of death	34,909	35,166	52,545
Birth date	54,188	52,052	73,702
Death date	53,606	52,299	73,833
Cause of death	2,198	4,161	5,821

Table 2: Extraction numbers

	Wikipedia	Wikidata	Shared
Origins	39,073	28,167	8,101
Professions	71,225	44,862	24,567
Place of death	17,379	17,636	17,530
Birth date	21,650	19,514	32,538
Death date	21,534	20,227	32,072
Cause of death	1,660	3,623	538

Table 3: Unique and shared extractions

professions and origins. The high numbers in professions are due to the fact that many persons have more than one. As an example, Wikidata lists six professions for the artist Kurt Cobain.

We also see that a perfect extractor would possibly find about 100% more causes of death on Wikipedia than we did in this paper. A large improvement could come from using more relations in dependency parsing and adding more search patterns to the extractor algorithm.

8 Analysis with a Database

We stored the resulting data in a SQL database with three tables: persons, origins, and profes-

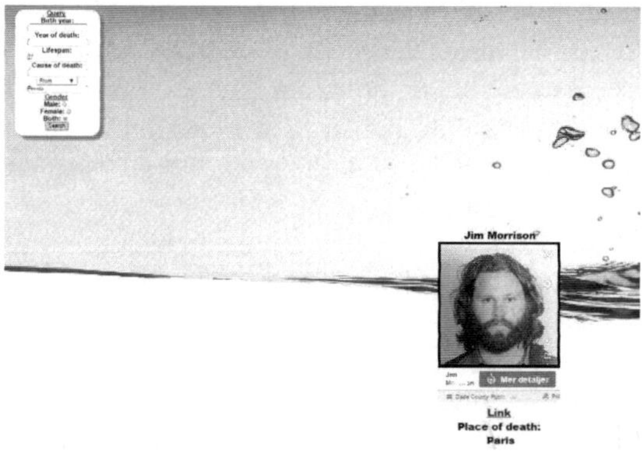

Figure 1: Screenshot of the interface

	Wikipedia	Wikidata	Both
Persons	–	79%	–
Origins	60%	59%	96%
Professions	123%	113%	180%
Place of death	45%	57%	67%
Birth date	69%	85%	94%
Death date	69%	85%	94%
Cause of death	3%	6.5%	7.5%

Table 4: Extraction ratios

sions. This separation was done since a person could have multiple values for both origin and profession.

We built a web application that we linked to the database and that enables a distant interaction with the system. A user can then query the system using a form and the results are presented as basic information about persons who matched the criteria with possible images and links to their Wikipedia page. Figure 1 shows an example of it.

The database can easily be queried to answer questions about our data. Table 5 shows, for instance, the most common causes of death.

Rank	Cause of death	Number of cases
1	Heart attack	885
2	Suicide	572
3	Execution	571
4	Stroke	333
5	Tuberculosis	296

Table 5: Top five causes of death

As discussed previously, the scores for professions and origins were high since persons could have multiple entries. With SQL, we could quickly check how many persons that we could connect to a profession and an origin. The result was 69,077 persons with one or more professions and 55,922 persons with one or more origins.

We also counted the number of unique property names and Table 6 shows the result.

Property	Number of unique cases
Cause of death	166
Profession	1,337
Origin	14,000
Place of death	10,106

Table 6: Unique properties

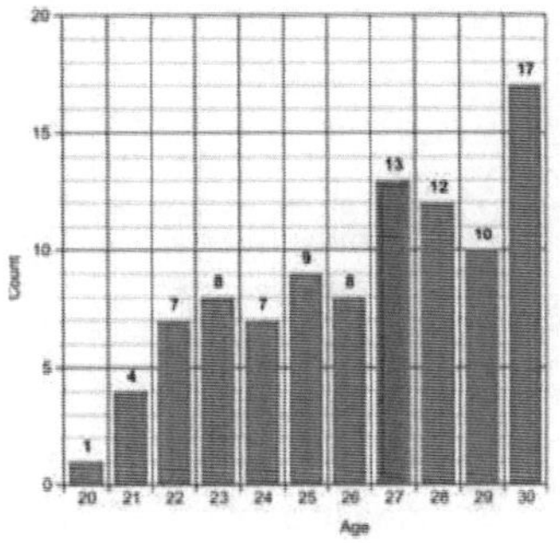

Figure 2: The death rate for musicians in the age range 20-30.

8.1 Evaluation of the Results on *Club 27*

Finally, to answer the initial question on the existence of a *Club 27*, the extractor produced a total number of 2,110 singers and musicians including many of the famous Club 27 members as Jimi Hendrix and Jim Morrison. Figure 2 shows the death count by age and this data could not support the existence of the Club 27 and, even if there is a spike at 27, more musicians died at 30...

The list of extracted musicians and singers in Table 7 can be compared with that in a page dedicated to Club 27 on the Swedish Wikipedia (Wikipedia, 2015). The latter contains 33 names, 34 with Jim Morrison, who was left out from the list, but mentioned in the text. Out of these 34 names, 19 did not have a Wikipedia page and were therefore ignored by our extractor. Out of the remaining 15 members, 11 were present in our list in Table 7. The four people our system did not find were:

- Alexandre Levy, pianist and composer
- Gary Thain, bassist
- Chris Bell, no dates of birth and death
- Richey James Edwards

Alexandre Levy existed in our database and was labeled as a pianist and composer. Gary Thain also existed with the profession of bassist. Both could have been included if we had broadened the definition of a musician to include the corresponding categories.

Chris Bell had neither birth or death date in his Swedish Wikipedia page and was thereby not included in our database.

Name	Gender	Born	Deceased	Death place
Jim Morrison	Male	1943-12-08	1971-07-03	Paris
Jimi Hendrix	Male	1942-11-27	1970-09-18	London
Kurt Cobain	Male	1967-02-20	1994-04-05	Seattle
Brian Jones	Male	1942-02-28	1969-07-03	Hartfield
Janis Joplin	Female	1943-01-19	1970-10-04	Los Angeles
Kristen Pfaff	Female	1967-05-26	1994-06-16	Seattle
Alan Wilson	Male	1943-07-04	1970-09-03	Topanga
Amy Winehouse	Female	1983-09-14	2011-07-23	London
Soledad Miranda	Female	1943-07-09	1970-08-18	Lisbon
Jeremy Michael Ward	Male	1976-05-05	2003-05-25	Los Angeles
Oskar Hoddø	Male	1916-01-01	1943-11-17	
Mia Zapata	Female	1965-08-25	1993-07-07	Seattle
Ron McKernan	Male	1945-09-08	1973-03-08	

Table 7: The members of Club 27 according to our extractor

Richey James Edwards on the other hand was marked as a musician, but was assigned a wrong year of death by the extractor. When analyzing his Wikipedia page, we could find the cause of this incorrect date: He was reported missing on February 1st, 1995 at 27 years old but his body was never found. He pronounced dead, much later, on November 23rd, 2008, which was the date the extractor collected and stored in the database.

We also found the two musicians, Soledad Miranda and Oskar Hoddø, that died at 27, but were not part of Wikipedia's list of Club 27.

9 Conclusion

In this paper, we described a system to combine data from a language-dependent information extraction system and a large semantic repository: Wikidata. Although the scope of the evaluation was limited, we showed that neither the extraction component, nor the repository could identify the complete set of facts we had in mind and that the interplay of both components significantly improved the final results.

We found that Wikidata was easy to integrate with a language-dependent pipeline and we believe that it has the potential to serve as a core semantic resource in many other information extraction applications.

Acknowledgments

This research was supported by Vetenskapsrådet through the *Det digitaliserade samhället* program.

References

Douglas Appelt, Jerry Hobbs, John Bear, David Israel, Megumi Kameyama, and Mabry Tyson. 1993. SRI: Description of the JV-FASTUS system used for MUC-5. In *Fifth Message Understanding Conference (MUC-5): Proceedings of a Conference Held in Baltimore, Maryland*, pages 221–235, San Francisco, August. Morgan Kaufmann.

Bliki. 2014. Bliki engine. bitbucket.org/axelclk/info.bliki.wiki/wiki/Home.

Sergey Chernov, Tereza Iofciu, Wolfgang Nejdl, and Xuan Zhou. 2006. Extracting semantic relationships between wikipedia categories. 1st International Workshop: SemWiki2006 – From Wiki to Semantics.

Hannes Dohrn and Dirk Riehle. 2013. Design and implementation of wiki content transformations and refactorings. In *Proceedings of the 9th International Symposium on Open Collaboration*, WikiSym '13, pages 2:1–2:10.

Yidong Fang. 2012. Json.simple. code.google.com/p/json-simple/.

Jerry R. Hobbs, Douglas E. Appelt, John Bear, David Israel, Megumi Kameyama, Mark Stickel, and Mabry Tyson. 1997. FASTUS: a cascaded finite-state transducer for extracting information from natural-language text. In Emmanuel Roche and Yves Schabes, editors, *Finite-State Language Processing*, chapter 13, pages 383–406. MIT Press, Cambridge, Massachusetts.

Dustin Lange, Christoph Böhm, and Felix Naumann. 2010. Extracting structured information from wikipedia articles to populate infoboxes. In *Proceedings of the 19th ACM International Conference on Information and Knowledge Management*, CIKM '10, pages 1661–1664.

Vivi Nastase and Michael Strube. 2008. Decoding wikipedia categories for knowledge acquisition. In *AAAI'08 Proceedings of the 23rd national conference on Artificial intelligence*, volume 2, pages 1219–1224.

Joakim Nivre, Johan Hall, and Jens Nilsson. 2006. Maltparser: A data-driven parser-generator for dependency parsing. In *Proceedings of LREC*.

Robert Östling. 2013. Stagger: an open-source part of speech tagger for Swedish. *Northern European Journal of Language Technology*, 3.

Wikipedia. 2015. Club 27. `http://sv.wikipedia.org/wiki/27_Club#Musiker_som_avlidit_vid_27_.C3.A5rs_.C3.A5lder`. Accessed March 11, 2015.

Fei Wu and Daniel S. Weld. 2007. Autonomously semantifying wikipedia. In *Proceedings of the Sixteenth ACM Conference on Conference on Information and Knowledge Management*, CIKM '07, pages 41–50.

Coarse-Grained Sense Annotation of Danish across Textual Domains

Sussi Olsen **Bolette S. Pedersen** **Héctor Martínez Alonso** **Anders Johannsen**
University of Copenhagen, Njalsgade 140, Copenhagen (Denmark)
{saolsen, bspedersen, alonso, ajohannsen}@hum.ku.dk

Abstract

We present the results of a coarse-grained sense annotation task on verbs, nouns and adjectives across six textual domains in Danish. We present the domain-wise differences in intercoder agreement and discuss how the applicability and validity of the sense inventory vary depending on domain. We find that domain-wise agreement is not higher in very canonical or edited text. In fact, newswire text and parliament speeches have lower agreement than blogs and chats, probably because the language of these text types is more complex and uses more abstract concepts. We further observe that domains differ in their sense distribution. For instance, newswire and magazines stand out as having a high focus on persons, and discussion fora typically include a restricted number of senses dependent on specialized topics. We anticipate that these findings can be exploited in automatic sense tagging when dealing with domain shift.

1 Introduction

It is commonly observed that word meanings vary substantially across textual domains, so that an appropriate sense inventory for one domain may be inappropriate or insufficient for another (Gale et al., 1992). This essential quality of the lexicon poses a huge challenge to natural language processing and underlines the need for developing systems that are generally less sensitive to domain shifts. The present work is framed within a project that deals with sense inventories of different granularity and across textual domains.

The overall goal is to discover what sense inventories and algorithms are manageable for annotation purposes and useful for automatic sense tagging. In this paper we experiment with coarse-grained annotations, and we analyze how reliable the annotations are and how much they vary over textual domains.

In Section 2 we present the backbone of our scalable sense inventory based on a monolingual dictionary of Danish. In Sections 3 and 4 we present the data, describing the different corpora, as well as the coarse-grained sense inventory. In Section 5 we present the differences in inter-coder agreement across the textual domains and discuss how the applicability and validity of the sense inventory vary depending on the kind of textual domain. Section 6 is devoted to comparisons of the relative frequency of selected supersenses across the six domains, and Section 7 describes the relation between specific senses via pointwise mutual information. Section 8 provides the conclusion for the article.

2 Scalable sense inventory

We operate with a sense inventory derived from the Danish wordnet (DanNet), which bases its sense inventory on a medium-sized Danish dictionary, Den Danske Ordbog (DDO). This is a pragmatic decision that leaves the more theoretical discussion aside of whether it is at all possible to define where one word sense starts and another begins (Kilgarriff, 2006). The ontological labels encoded in DanNet, based on the EuroWordNet top ontology as described in Pedersen et al. (2009) and Vossen (1998), have enabled us to automatically the word senses defined for the Danish vocabulary onto the cross-lingual supersenses. These are based on the Princeton Wordnet lexicographical classes[1] and have become a popular choice for coarse-grained sense tagging with the advantage of being applicable across languages.

[1] https://wordnet.princeton.edu/man/lexnames.5WN.html

Sussi Olsen, Bolette S. Pedersen, Héctor Martínez Alonso and Anders Johannsen 2015. Coarse-grained sense annotation of Danish across textual domains. *Proceedings of the workshop on Semantic resources and semantic annotation for Natural Language Processing and the Digital Humanities at NODALIDA 2015.* NEALT Proceedings Series 27 / Linköping Electronic Conference Proceedings 112: 36–43.

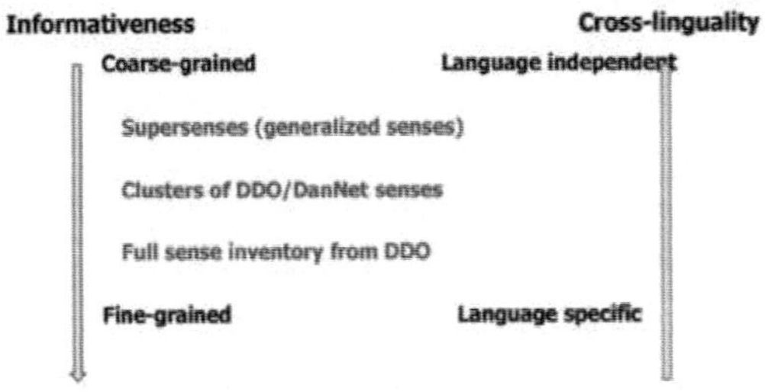

Figure 1: Scales of sense granularity.

All corpora have been automatically pre-annotated on the basis of this mapping, allowing the annotator to choose the appropriate supersense in context.

Figure 1 shows three points on the continuum of word sense granularity applied in the project, spanning from the supersense annotation experiment presented in this paper over clusters of DDO senses, to the highly fine-grained full sense inventory of DDO applied to lexical samples experiments (Pedersen et al., 2015).

3 Corpora across domains

In this paper we use the term *domain* (or textual domain) for text type or genre, and not for subject domain; i.e. our domains are categories like BLOG, CHAT, and MAGAZINE, instead of Politics, Geography or Literature. The texts for annotation have been selected from the Danish CLARIN Reference Corpus (Asmussen and Halskov, 2012), which is a general-language corpus of 45M words spanning several text types or domains, although with a predominance of newswire texts (48%) . We have taken care to include a broad range of domains in our annotation data set.

Table 1 lists the domains and text sources that have been selected for manual annotation from each domain. The rightmost column shows the names of the domains in this paper.

3.1 Corpus characteristics

We have characterized aspects of language use in the different textual domains with regard to average sentence length and the token/type ratio. The results of the analysis can be seen in Table 2.

Average sentence length is considerably larger for PARLIAMENT. These texts are originally speeches, written down by professional secretary staff, and long sentences are common in this genre. Apart from this, differences in sentence length between the textual domains are small. We initially expected the texts produced by professionals (NEWSWIRE and MAGAZINE) to have longer sentences than user-generated texts (BLOG, CHAT and FORUM), but found that for the user-generated content domains the language was similar to spoken language, and punctuation was less used, which may account for the longer sentences.

Domain	Av. sent.length	$\frac{\text{token}}{\text{type}}$	# sentences
BLOG	19.83	3.88	600
FORUM	22.22	3.22	300
CHAT	18.66	3.83	600
MAGAZINE	20.58	2.90	600
PARLIAMENT	32.49	5.07	600
NEWSWIRE	19.47	2.66	600

Table 2: Language characteristics of the textual domains.

The token/type ratio measures the variety of the vocabulary, or more precisely the average number of repetitions of each type. A higher token/type ratio thus means a less varied choice of vocabulary. PARLIAMENT is the domain with the highest token/type ratio. The domains BLOG and CHAT also have a rather high token/type ratio, which fits well with the annotators' impression that the language in these textual domains was homogenous with lots of repetitions. We find the highest lexical variation in the newswire domain.

3.2 Annotation process

The texts in our analyses were manually annotated by trained students. Our students annotate using WebAnno, a web-based annotation tool developed by Technische Universität Darmstadt for the CLARIN community (Yimam et al., 2013). Using WebAnno allows monitoring and measuring the progress and the quality of the annotation projects in terms of inter-annotator agreement.

More than half of the sentences have been annotated by two or more annotators in order to measure inter-annotator agreement, and most of these sentences have been adjudicated by a trained linguist. The remaining sentences have only been annotated by one annotator. Three annotators worked on the newswire texts, and two of them did the annotations on the remaining texts. Although these two annotators are skilled and, as demonstrated by the adjudication process, adhered closely to the instruction guidelines, the low num-

Source	Description	Domain
Bentes blog	A blog written by a woman in her forties	BLOG
Selvhenter	A chat forum mostly used by young people	CHAT
Se og Hør	A celebrity gossip magazine	MAGAZINE
Folketingstaler	Speeches from the Danish Parliament written down by professionals	PARLIAMENT
Mangamania	A chat forum for persons who love manga	FORUM
Politiken	A large Danish newspaper	NEWSWIRE

Table 1: The domains and texts included in the annotation data set.

ber of annotators may have adversely affected the results, leading to slightly biased data (see Section 5).

4 The extended supersense inventory

Basing the supersense inventory on the Princeton Wordnet lexicographical classes has the advantage of being inter-lingually comparable and interoperable, because wordnets for a wide range of languages are linked to Princeton Wordnet.

However, the supersense classes were not originally designed for sense annotation. During the annotation process, we discovered that some senses are needlessly coarse and in fact confound important distinctions. Therefore, we refine the Princeton supersense inventory with additional senses in cases where these cover large groups of easily detectable word senses in DanNet, such as diseases, body parts, institutions and vehicles. Because this is a process of refinement, we maintain compatibility with Princeton Wordnet. A new sense is introduced by subdividing an original sense and can thus always be unambiguously mapped back to the original sense.The full set of supersenses with the extensions can be seen in Table 3.

In total, the standard supersense set has been extended with seven noun categories and two verb categories. For adjectives, which only have a *catch-all* sense in Princeton Wordnet, we have added four high-level categories covering mental, social, physical and time-related property senses. The inspiration for the new adjective senses came from the four major sense groupings from the Danish wordnet. Finally, three tags for verbal satellites have been introduced to account for collocations, particles, and reflexive pronouns. While these satellite tags seemingly do not carry semantic meaning but are more grammatical in nature, they obtain a semantic interpretation in conjunction with a verb. In particular they ensure that a certain particle, pronoun or element of a collocation is understood as a lexical unit in conjunction with its preceding verb. To exemplify, Figure 2 shows how the phrasal verb *sige fra* (lit. say from, ‘cancel’) receives the supersense verb.communication, while the particle fra received the particle tag.

Figure 2: Annotation of phrasal verbs.

Ide and Wilks (2006), Brown et al. (2010) and more recently Melo et al. (2012) discuss coarse-grained sense distinctions for natural language processing, and Ciaramita and Johnson (2003) provide one of the first to use lexicographical classes as sense inventory for an automatic prediction task.

5 Inter-annotator agreement across domains

Over 50% of our data, 1900 sentences in total, has been doubly annotated with the aim of measuring and controlling annotator consistency. The disagreements inform on the validity of the sense inventory in general as well as for the different domains. They also provide hints about problematic, document-specific issues. Such issues were found for BLOG, for instance, which includes a frequent number of meta remarks where a certain feed can be found, as in:

> *Dette indlæg blev udgivet den tirsdag, 21. september 2010 kl. 10:14 og er gemt i Min have. Du kan følge alle svar til dette indlæg via RSS 2.0-feedet. (Bentes Blog)*

ADJ.ALL	NOUN.FOOD	**SAT.PARTICLE**
ADJ.MENTAL	NOUN.GROUP	**SAT.RELFPRON**
ADJ.PHYS	**NOUN.INSTITUTION**	VERB.ACT
ADJ.SOCIAL	NOUN.LOCATION	**VERB.ASPECTUAL**
ADJ.TIME	NOUN.MOTIVE	VERB.BODY
NOUN.TOPS	NOUN.OBJECT	VERB.CHANGE
NOUN.ABSTRACT	NOUN.PERSON	VERB.COGNITION
NOUN.ACT	NOUN.PHENOMENON	VERB.COMMUNICATION
NOUN.ANIMAL	NOUN.PLANT	VERB.COMPETITION
NOUN.ARTIFACT	NOUN.POSSESSION	VERB.CONSUMPTION
NOUN.ATTRIBUTE	NOUN.PROCESS	VERB.CONTACT
NOUN.BODY	NOUN.QUANTITY	VERB.CREATION
NOUN.BUILDING	NOUN.RELATION	VERB.EMOTION
NOUN.COGNITION	NOUN.SHAPE	VERB.MOTION
NOUN.COMMUNICATION	NOUN.STATE	VERB.PERCEPTION
NOUN.CONTAINER	NOUN.SUBSTANCE	**VERB.PHENOMENON**
NOUN.DISEASE	NOUN.TIME	VERB.POSSESSION
NOUN.DOMAIN	**NOUN.VEHICLE**	VERB.SOCIAL
NOUN.FEELING	**SAT.COLL**	VERB.STATIVE

Table 3: The standard supersense inventory with the added senses/satellite types in bold.

Domain	κ-agreement	% double annotated
BLOG	0.66	50 %
FORUM	0.54	66 %
CHAT	0.68	66 %
MAGAZINE	0.61	33 %
PARLIAMENT	0.59	33 %
NEWSWIRE	0.59	100 %
All domains	0.63	

Table 4: Inter-annotator agreement κ across domains together with the percentage of double annotated files.

> This feed was published Tuesday September 21 at 10:00 and is saved under My garden. You can follow all comments to this feed via the RSS 2.0 feed.

In such cases the annotators reached a consensus on how to tag the blog-specific metadata.

Table 4 shows that even if agreement results are generally good for the task (Artstein and Poesio, 2008), not all textual domains are equally easy to annotate. NEWSWIRE and PARLIAMENT show the lowest agreement, which is a somewhat surprising finding, because these texts are the most canonical and elaborate and thus arguably easier to understand and annotate. FORUM has 300 sentences, unlike the other domains, which have double the amount. This difference has an impact in the chance-correction measure of the κ coefficient, making the chance-adjustment more severe. However, NEWSWIRE has more semantic types than e.g. BLOG (see Figure 3, 4 and 5), and the more varied the text, the more difficult it will be to annotate and achieve high agreement. Furthermore, PARLIAMENT texts are in a higher register than texts from BLOG or CHAT and include more abstract words (verb.cognition, noun.abstract).

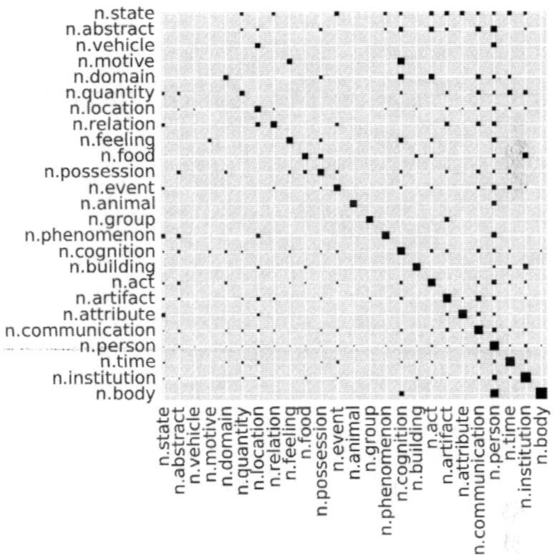

Figure 3: Disagreement for noun senses in NEWSWIRE.

Figures 3 to 5 illustrate the patterns of disagreement between annotators. The matrix is constructed by first gathering all of the words tagged by at least one annotator as, say, noun.abstract, observing what the other annotators tagged the same words as. Each cell in the plotted matrix measures the number of times two annotators tagged

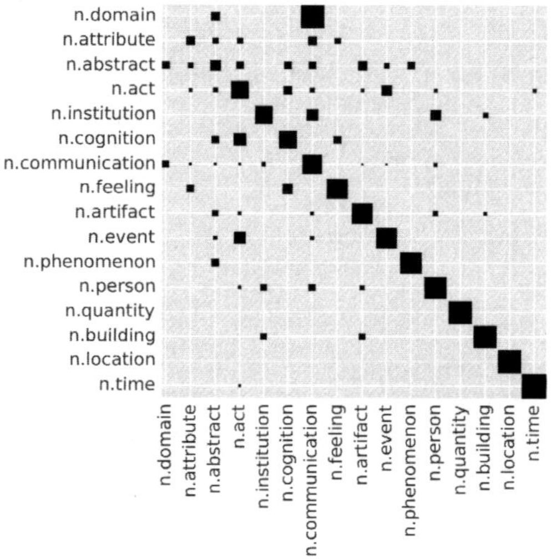

Figure 4: Disagreement for noun senses in BLOG.

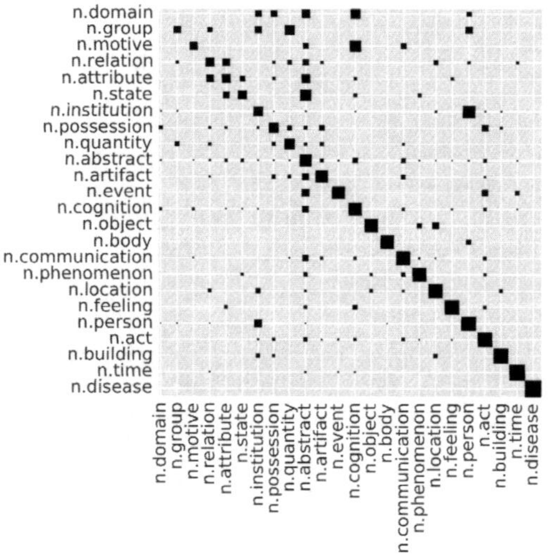

Figure 5: Disagreement for noun senses in PARLIAMENT.

Word	Conflicting annotation
musik (music)	noun.communication
dans (dancing)	noun.act
natradio (night radio)	noun.communication
design (design)	noun.attribute
kultur (culture)	noun.cognition

Table 5: Examples of disagreement between noun.domain and another supersense.

a word with a given combination of tags (e.g. one annotator chose noun.abstract and another chose noun.body). Large entries on the diagonal indicate agreement, while off-diagonal entries mean that two senses are confused. Furthermore, the matrix is normalized by row, and rows are sorted after the size of the diagonal value. Thus the senses with the worst disagreement appear first while the best senses are located near the bottom of the matrix.

For instance, the sense noun.group has a smaller value in the diagonal than in the column for noun.quantity. This difference indicates that annotators often disagree about these senses, and that there is little agreement on when to assign the sense noun.group. Other senses like noun.food have perfect or near-perfect agreement. In all three disagreement plots, covering the NEWSWIRE, BLOG and PARLIAMENT, we find that the supersense noun.domain is problematic to the annotators. This supersense has a smaller value in the diagonal than in the column for communication and cognition.

Table 5 shows some examples of this disagreement, where nouns have been annotated with noun.domain and some other sense respectively. As a consequence this supersense should either be better explained and exemplified in the annotator guidelines, or it should be discarded from the extended list altogether.

We also observe that some of the very frequently used types are easier to annotate in NEWSWIRE than in BLOG and PARLIAMENT debates. This is true for supersenses such as noun.institution and noun.communication (for supersense frequency see Section 6) where the number of off-diagonal boxes are lower for NEWSWIRE than for the other textual domains. More metaphorical language in political speeches, which is generally harder to annotate, could explain this difference, as well as frequent reference

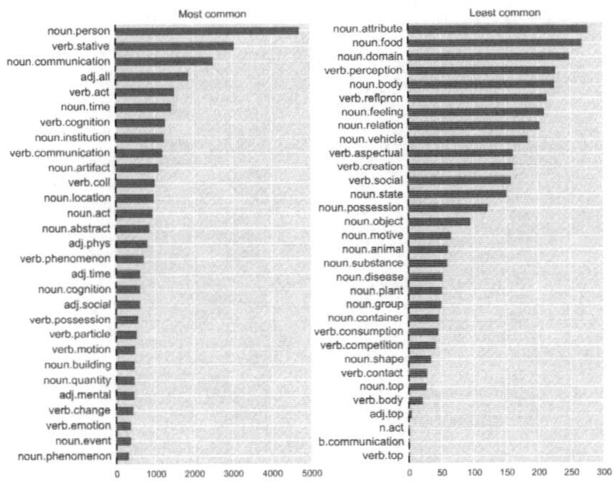

Figure 6: Most and least frequent supersenses in the complete annotated corpus.

Sense 1	Sense 2	PMI
verb.consumption	noun.food	2.71
verb.contact	noun.body	2.26
noun.food	noun.container	2.04
verb.body	noun.body	1.39
noun.disease	noun.body	1.29
verb.competition	noun.event	1.13
verb.motion	verb.contact	1.10
verb.contact	noun.artifact	1.08
noun.substance	noun.object	1.07
noun.shape	noun.body	1.06
noun.vehicle	noun.substance	0.79
verb.competition	noun.relation	0.75

Table 6: Mutual information for supersenses.

to institutions of a very different status.

6 Sense distributions

We now analyze the variation across domains for the top 15 supersenses. Figure 7 provides a picture of which senses are the dominating in each selected domain compared to the sense distribution in the complete annotated corpus in Figure 6.

We observe that noun.person is by far the most frequent tag in MAGAZINE and NEWSWIRE where references to people make up a large portion of the text. The MAGAZINE domain is mostly tabloid content in which the life of famous people is discussed. In contrast, the annotated blogs refer only sparingly to people but focus on personal reflections on life. The tag noun.communication is frequent in BLOG, partly influenced by the meta comments exemplified in Section 5.

The CHAT domain is the only one where the first most frequent sense is not a nominal sense, but instead the verb.stative supersense (mainly forms of the verb *være*, to be). In this domain pronominal subjects are about three times as common as in the NEWSWIRE domain, and many of the syntactic slots (e.g. subject) that would otherwise be satisfied by noun.person in other types of text are satisfied by pronouns in this domain. This explains why noun.person is only the fourth most frequent sense in this domain.

In FORUM, noun.artifact is the second most frequent sense, because the members of the forum discuss *things*: publications, computer parts, and collectible card games. More abstract concepts like movies or games are often referred to in their physical incarnation. The high frequency of noun.artifact is a result of the specialized topic of the forum.

The PARLIAMENT texts are special in several ways, which we see reflected in the annotations. Abstract concepts and verbal states are frequent for this text type, which is not the case for the other text types. Moreover, this text type has more words per sentence and the highest token/type ratio (as seen in Table 2) and thus the least varied language.

7 Relation between senses

This section offers an overview on how supersenses co-occur. To give account for relevant associations between senses, we use PMI (pointwise mutual information), which is an information-theoretical measure of association between variables. Higher PMI values indicate stronger association, i.e. variable A is more predictable from variable B.

Table 6 shows the twelve pairs of supersense with the highest pointwise mutual information calculated across sentences. We observe that some of the associations are prototypical selectional restrictions like verb.comsumption + noun.food as in:

> *Hvad drikker I af sodavand , hvis I gør?*
> What kind of soda (noun.food) do you drink(verb.consumption), if you do?

Other associations are topical, regardless of parts of speech, like verb.competition and noun.event:

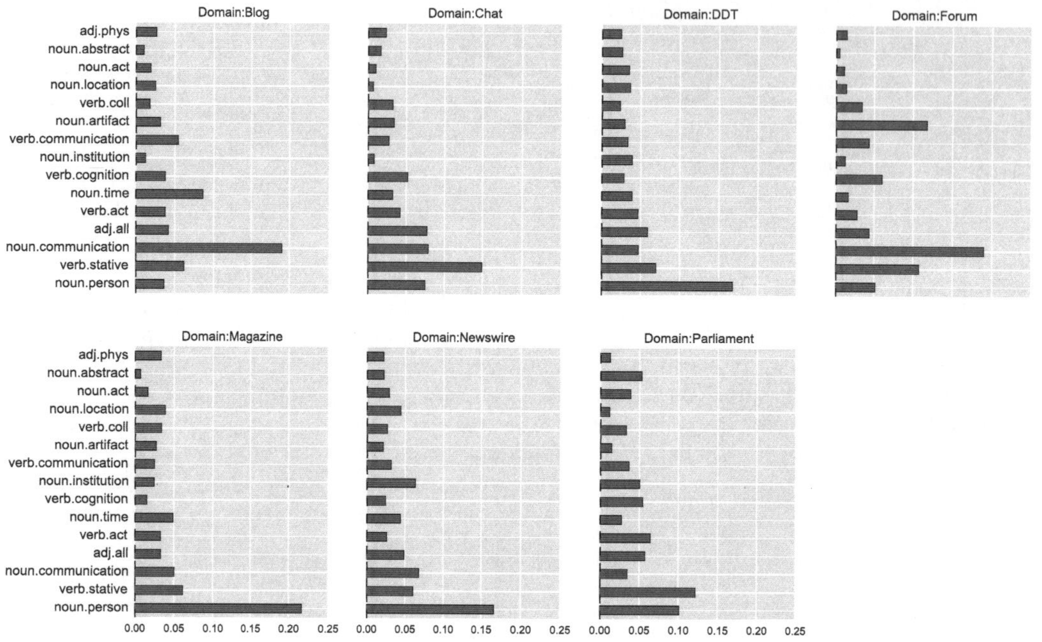

Figure 7: Variation across domains in the top 15 supersenses.

FCK har vundet pokalfinalen.
FCK has won(verb.competition) the cup final(noun.event).

Finally, some of the associations appear for the same part of speech, like noun.disease and noun.body, or noun.food and noun.container. In these associations, one sense is a strong indicator for the other at the topic level (diseases are bodily; food is kept somewhere, etc).

8 Conclusion

We observe that domain-wise agreement is not linked to factors such as how canonical the text is, and whether the text is professionally edited or not. The NEWSWIRE and PARLIAMENT domains, which contain the most thoroughly edited text in the corpus, have the lowest agreement, which is somewhat unexpected. Here we suggest that certain words and sense variations are intrinsically more difficult, e.g. abstract senses. In comparison, FORUM has a clear topic, constraining the discourse elements and their semantic type and thus making annotation easier.

The annotation task yields good agreement for supersense annotations across a number of domains, matching or exceeding the level of agreement found in previous, comparable studies. However, a few supersenses are hard to apply uniformly across all domains, calling for further analysis and perhaps an adjustment of the sense inventory. Abstract noun supersenses as well as verb supersenses related to cognition were generally harder to annotate consistently than more concrete supersenses.

By examining the top 15 supersenses of each domain, we have also shown how textual domains differ in their sense distribution. These observations can later be exploited in automatic sense tagging when dealing with domain shift. One way to do this is pre-estimating the most-frequent sense of the target domain using a lexical knowledge base like DanNet.

For experiments with automatic tagging of Danish data based on the annotations, we refer to Martínez Alonso et al. (2015a) and Martínez Alonso et al. (2015b).

Acknowledgements

We wish to thank the anonymous reviewers for their valuable comments. Likewise, we thank all the project staff, as well as our team of annotators.

The research resulting in this publication has been funded by the Danish Research Council under the *Semantic Processing across Domains* project: `http://cst.ku.dk/english/projekter/semantikprojekt/`.

References

Ron Artstein and Massimo Poesio. 2008. Inter-coder agreement for computational linguistics. *Computational Linguistics*, 34(4):555–596.

Jørg Asmussen and Jakob Halskov. 2012. The CLARIN DK Reference Corpus. In *Sprogteknologisk Workshop*.

Susan Windisch Brown, Travis Rood, and Martha Palmer. 2010. Number or nuance: Which factors restrict reliable word sense annotation? In *LREC*.

Massimiliano Ciaramita and Mark Johnson. 2003. Supersense tagging of unknown nouns in wordnet. In *Proceedings of the 2003 conference on Empirical methods in natural language processing*, pages 168–175. Association for Computational Linguistics.

Gerard De Melo, Collin F Baker, Nancy Ide, Rebecca J Passonneau, and Christiane Fellbaum. 2012. Empirical comparisons of masc word sense annotations. In *LREC*, pages 3036–3043.

William A Gale, Kenneth W Church, and David Yarowsky. 1992. One sense per discourse. In *Proceedings of the workshop on Speech and Natural Language*, pages 233–237. Association for Computational Linguistics.

Nancy Ide and Yorick Wilks. 2006. Making sense about sense. In *Word sense disambiguation*, pages 47–73. Springer.

Adam Kilgarriff. 2006. Word senses. In Eneko Agirre and Philip Edmonds, editors, *Word Sense Disambiguation*, pages 29–46. Springer.

Héctor Martínez Alonso, Anders Johannsen, Anders Søgaard, Sussi Olsen, Anna Braasch, Sanni Nimb, Nicolai Hartvig Sørensen, and Bolette Sandford Pedersen. 2015a. Supersense tagging for danish. In *Nodalida*.

Héctor Martínez Alonso, Barbara Plank, Anders Johannsen, and Søgaard. 2015b. Active learning for sense annotation. In *Nodalida*.

Bolette Sandford Pedersen, Sanni Nimb, Jørg Asmussen, Nicolai Hartvig Sørensen, Lars Trap-Jensen, and Henrik Lorentzen. 2009. Dannet: the challenge of compiling a wordnet for danish by reusing a monolingual dictionary. *Language resources and evaluation*, 43(3):269–299.

Bolette Pedersen, Anna Braasch, Sanni Nimb, and Sussi Olsen. 2015. Betydningsinventar - i ordbøger og i løbende tekst, forthcoming. In *Presentation at the 13th Conference on Lexicography in the Nordic Countries*.

Piek Vossen. 1998. *EuroWordNet: A multilingual database with lexical semantic networks*. Springer.

Seid Muhie Yimam, Iryna Gurevych, Richard Eckart de Castilho, and Chris Biemann. 2013. Webanno: A flexible, web-based and visually supported system for distributed annotations. In *ACL (Conference System Demonstrations)*, pages 1–6.